"An utterly engaging book that offers practical advice for managers at all levels. If you want to be a better manager – keep this little book handy and refer to it often."
Ranulph Fiennes, Expedition Leader and Writer

"With this 'little black book' on their desk, managers' confidence should be restored."
Major General Patrick Cordingley, Commander of the Desert Rats in the first Gulf War

"Practical examples and thoughtful analysis – this book is what it says on the cover: a handbook, to be kept at your side and referred to often."
Steve Maine, TMT Chief Executive

"*The Little Black Book for Managers* is written in a delightful style which encompasses the authors' wide experience, practical approach, assertive manner, and above all their original and inspirational style. It should be required reading for aspiring or ambitious managers in every field."
Lt-Gen Sir Robin Ross KCB, OBE, former Commandant-General, Royal Marines

"Bridges academic research, experience and knowledge into something that truly provides managers and leaders with useful, tangible advice, converting the complex into the simple. Brilliant."
Richard Knight OBE, Operations Director, Newcastle International Airport

"I would challenge anyone who has been a manager not to have a wry smile when reading and recognising themselves in these situations."
Caroline Evans, Learning & Development Manager, Marshall Aerospace

"At last! This great little no-nonsense new book fills the yawning gap that, in my opinion, has existed for decades within the management training armoury."
Malcolm Diamond MBE, Chairman, Trifast plc

"Management is more art than science. This *Little Black Book* invites the reader to develop their own management art through observation, experience, openness and personal authenticity. Dip in here and there, or dive in for total immersion. Either way, use it again and again to hone your management performance."
Paul Burfitt, former Global CIO, AstraZeneca plc

"Every senior manager at Fugro has had the benefit of training by John and his team. The core of John's message is well captured in *The Little Black Book for Managers*. Uncluttered and easy to follow, the material is readily accessible and effective for use by managers in their daily life. "
Paul van Riel, Chairman, Fugro nv

"A very worthwhile book that will benefit every management student, as well as providing straightforward and valuable advice to managers facing real challenges in their demanding roles both now and in the future."
John Steele, former Group Personnel Director, BT plc

"A remarkable book about managing people and objectives. I loved it."
Sir Peter Bonfield, CBE, FREng

"This is not like most management books you will have read or have on your shelves. There's at least one challenge, two interesting management stories, and three options to think about on every page. Not always comfortable – seeing how often I could have done something better – but a lot of gems in one concise volume."
Clive Ansell, CEO, Systems & Applications, Tribal Group plc

"Like the yucca plant, this book is such a joy that I suspect it will soon be seen in every manager's office!"
Geoff Burch, Writer and Conference Speaker

"Smashingly insightful – John, Rafael and Kevin have captured in these few pages what many of us have taken four decades to learn through experience and trial and error."
Phil Stutes, Regional Manager Americas, Fugro Survey

"Whether you are just starting your managerial career, in the middle or at the top of your profession, *The Little Black Book for Managers* is an essential reference for all."
Stewart Davies, Managing Partner MLC50LLP

"An influential and valuable work that combines management theory with practical experiences."
Ray Wood CEng, MBA, Executive Vice President

"Valuable advice on how to inspire your staff and manage more successfully."
Steve Morgan OBE, Chairman, Redrow plc

"Managers at all levels looking for ways to improve performance will find here a wealth of accessible nuggets drawn from practical experience across many companies and sectors."
Sir Peter Norriss, KBE, CB, AFC, former Air Force Board member, Chairman and Non-executive Director

"Some intriguing and powerful ideas. Easy to recall advice – and the stories it contains makes it fun to read."
Martin Hess, Vice President, HP Enterprise Services

"A guide and resource for creative managers who want to achieve more."
Pieter van Oord, CEO Van Oord b.v., Dredging and Marine Contractors

© 2013 John Cross, Rafael Gomez and Kevin Money

Moments of power is a registered trademark owned by John Cross

Registered office

John Wiley and Sons Ltd, The Atrium, Southern Gate, Chichester, West Sussex, PO19 8SQ, United Kingdom

For details of our global editorial offices, for customer services and for information about how to apply for permission to reuse the copyright material in this book please see our website at www.wiley.com.

The right of the authors to be identified as the authors of this work has been asserted in accordance with the Copyright, Designs and Patents Act 1988.

Reprinted October 2013

Library of Congress Cataloging-in-Publication Data

Cross, John, 1947–
  The little black book for managers: how to maximize your key management moments of power / John Cross, Rafael Gomez, Kevin Money.
    pages cm
  Includes bibliographical references and index.
  ISBN 978-1-118-74423-9 (hardback) – ISBN 978-1-118-74422-2 (ebk) – ISBN 978-1-118-74419-2 (ebk)   1. Decision making.   2. Management.   I. Gomez, Rafael, 1972–   II. Money, Kevin, 1972–   III. Title.
    HD30.23.C76 2013
    658.4'03–dc23

2013027320

A catalogue record for this book is available from the British Library.

ISBN 978-1-118-74423-9 (hbk)   ISBN 978-1-118-74422-2 (ebk)
ISBN 978-1-118-74419-2 (ebk)

Set in 10/12.5 pt Rotis Sans Serif Std by Toppan Best-set Premedia Limited

Cover design by Parent Design Ltd

Printed in Great Britain by TJ International Ltd, Padstow, Cornwall, UK

THE LITTLE BLACK BOOK FOR MANAGERS

HOW TO MAXIMIZE YOUR KEY MANAGEMENT MOMENTS OF POWER ®

John Cross, Rafael Gomez,
and Kevin Money

CAPSTONE
A Wiley Brand

CONTENTS

FOREWORD

Hello, I'm John. I started writing this book primarily for my three grown-up children. They have progressed well in their careers and have become managers, responsible for the performance of others; but none has ever received any meaningful training or development to help them understand the roles and responsibilities of a manager. Nor have they received any advice in dealing with common situations they find at work. Unfortunately, their situation is not at all uncommon.

Separately, as the Chief Executive of iSolon Limited for the past 13 years, I have been designing learning and development programmes for major corporations and delivering them around the world. Although the objectives of each programme have varied widely, the main content has tended to focus upon leadership and management issues.

This book, then, is an attempt to help every manager, including my children, deal with the challenges that each day brings. It combines the lessons I have learned the hard way, with material that I have quoted from others who have inspired me through their books, articles and analysis, with advice gained by listening to those far wiser than me.

For the past dozen years or so, I have read almost every issue of the *Harvard Business Review* and *McKinsey Quarterly* and scoured the pages of the *Financial Times* for management analysis and insight. All three publications have proved enormously valuable to me.

The result is that after more than 12 months of writing (and a lifetime of learning), I offer to you my personal management and leadership insights. Each of the recommendations, techniques and models that I suggest are frequently interdependent or mutually reinforcing and are therefore designed to be added to the previous ones.

WHY YOU SHOULD READ THIS BOOK

Imagine this: You've just settled into your airline seat and told to "relax and enjoy the flight." No chance – but wait, the pilot has another announcement. "Ladies and Gentlemen, this is a very proud day for me because I'm looking forward to making my first take-off and landing. My boss has told me that because of my work on compiling the company's health and safety manual, I would make a good pilot. So here I am. I start my training next year – but the boss thought it would be a good idea to throw me in at the deep end and see how I get on. Now – where's the ignition key?"

They don't let you loose with a couple of hundred passengers and a $30m aircraft without proper training, a licence from the regulatory authorities and periodic ability checks by your peers. But it seems OK to give someone a dozen people of mixed abilities, ages and ethnicity; a number of activities to complete; a set of company processes, procedures and quality standards; a set of team objectives and key performance targets; and a budget. Suck it and see! No problem!

Pilots train and re-train constantly and undergo periodic capability checks. Sadly, the vast majority of managers don't, and yet the story of Captain Sully, the US Airlines pilot who safely landed his plane on the Hudson River[1]*, is testament to the power of ongoing training and regular capability checks.

Being a manager is a profession, like being a pilot, doctor or accountant is a profession. But when promoted to manage pilots, doctors or accountants, I believe people should re-train in their new role. Yes – knowledge of flying, medicine or International Financial Reporting Standards will help, but they are not the primary responsibility. So, whatever your technical discipline, your primary responsibility, or "profession", is management.

This book is your handy practical "toolkit" or "field guide" to management. It is designed so that you can "dip in and dip out" to self-check your preference for a particular course of action against an alternative. You can use it also to maximize the benefit from situations when you can have the most impact, because it contains the tools and techniques to leverage those opportunities and avoid potential risks. Some of the tools and techniques won't fit your situation precisely, but neither can the rich kaleidoscope of "How To" leadership and management book models that are offered. They can't. But a few of the tools I offer for your consideration might fit well enough to make your life a little bit easier and a little bit more rewarding. Which ones? Only you can tell.

You might notice that there are some deliberate contradictions. Why? Because there is no "one size fits all" in management. Different personalities, when in exactly the same circumstances, may need different management handling. People from different cultures will respond differently to a universal management style.

You may instinctively agree with some of my recommendations and yet reject others. But whether you agree with it or not, aim to put the advice into your specific context and culture and twist

*Please refer to our *Further Reading* section on page 201.

it into a shape that is compatible with your circumstances, personality and prejudices.

During the process of writing, Kevin Money and Rafael Gomez kindly agreed to help me. Their deep understanding of the economic motives and underlying psychology of much of what is recommended for the reader to consider, means that the following advice is supported not only from the experiences of literally hundreds of managers, but is also in line with the latest academic thinking. However, we have decided to retain the first person singular style as we all believe that you will benefit more from a private and confidential style.

HOW TO USE THIS BOOK

This is not a "beginning, middle and end" type of book. The book is structured in terms of the events and personal interactions that form an essential part of a manager's life – from setting objectives, to managing a meeting with colleagues and appraising the performance of others – so you can immediately access the help you need.

Part 1 – "Your Rewarding Job" is all about the main aspects of your job, such as setting objectives and targets; you'll find methods to help you modularize workflow patterns and identify possible areas for improvement. I will emphasize the importance of collecting and maintaining accurate and up-to-date performance data, and show how to respond to requests for time and money estimates.

Part 2 – "It's All About You" is all about you, the manager, where you can examine your strengths and weaknesses; the kind of example you will set to your colleagues and the decisions you make about how to spend your time; and how to avoid undermining yourself, and thereby diminish your power to influence and persuade others.

Part 3 — "Your Team is What You Make it" is all about the people that work with and under you. You'll learn how to incentivize them to exceed previous achievements; how to improve your team's ratings from supplier and customer groups; how to maximize the benefit of team meetings; and how to deal with the big issues that face you and your colleagues.

Part 4 — "Your Talented Staff" is all about individual team members; finding out how to leverage their individual talents and mitigate their weaknesses; how to get them to understand and appreciate the talents of their colleagues; how to recruit a new team member and how to upskill your team by asking a poor performer to leave. Most importantly, I will ask you to be flexible enough to allow some of your people total freedom while others are closely monitored.

KEEP THIS BOOK HANDY FOR FUTURE REFERENCE

Why? Because tomorrow you will be faced with at least one of the situations described in the book and you may feel all alone with the problem. Who will you turn to for advice? Have others been in the same or similar circumstances as you and what did they do? If this book is kept handy, a re-reading of a similar, if not identical, situation may help you to plan the way forward more effectively or give you more options to consider. I'd be surprised if you aren't feeling challenged by one or more of the scenarios present in the book right now! Scenarios such as:

- A tricky, awkward or threatening situation.
- A lack of confidence to deal with other people in the way that is needed.
- The need to assert your authority more.
- Awarding fair bonuses.
- The need for guidance on how to admonish your team members or punish misbehaviour.

- How to get extra effort from your team; guidance on how best to incentivize.
- A feeling of powerlessness.
- The realization that you need to delegate more.
- A desire to manage your time more effectively.
- Having to deal with underperformers on your team.
- Having to deal with conflict between team members, or between teams.

You might feel that you have dealt with these challenges effectively before, yet still benefit from the offer of additional or even contradictory options. In many examples, I recommend specific phrases or sentences that you will find helpful.

Keep *The Little Black Book for Managers* handy for reference. It may be the only help you get.

INTRODUCTION

WHAT ARE "KEY MOMENTS OF POWER"?

In every manager's career there are moments where personal choices are critical in bringing about either success or failure. The trick is to identify *each of these situations and in doing so, maximize the positives and reduce the negatives.* This book will help you to understand your moments of power as a manager by helping you identify those moments when you can have the biggest impact, the moments when you could make the wrong choices, the moments when you will have dilemmas. The advice offered applies equally to managers operating in every industry, from wildcat oil and gas exploration company managers working offshore in hostile conditions, to production-line supervisors working in a chocolate factory. The advice, backed up by academic research, is based on thousands of personal experiences and, as a result, is full of practical insights.

Moments of power occur to everyone, every day. Even making room for another motorist to change lanes is a moment of power. At work, moments of power occur regularly too, but with the vast majority of managers failing to recognize them. My aim is to bring these moments into your immediate consciousness and get you to store them for later retrieval so that when they next occur, later today or next year, you pause to reflect on their potential to improve your authority, your status, your enjoyment of the job and perhaps on the respect that your team has for you.

The Little Black Book for Managers has been conceived and designed as an independent support tool for managers at all levels, from shop-floor supervisor to main board director. While it will be particularly useful for newly appointed managers, it is equally powerful for managers with vast experience who may benefit from being reminded of some of the fundamental principles.

When you get into the habit of recognizing and leveraging your moments of power, then not only will you be better off, your team members, your colleagues and your bosses will be as well. Quite a promise I know, so let me give you three examples from real-life experiences:

Moment of Power – Example 1

"If you always do what you've always done, you'll always get the same outcome."

Jane has to choose three accountants to conduct the audit of her most annoying client. She has to choose from a bank of 14 of varying abilities. For the past three years, the client had been critical of both the process and the findings.

The moment of power in this true story appears obvious, doesn't it? Answer – choose the three with the highest ability and incentivize them to achieve the best ever customer satisfaction rating. Job done, time to move on to the next issue. But to illustrate the core principle of the book, let's pause and create some alternative options for this particular moment of power.

- **Option 1** – Decline the client's invitation to conduct the audit.
- **Option 2** – Jane to complete the audit personally with two assistants.

- **Option 3** – Jane mentally categorizes the client as "difficult", retains her best three accountants for more appreciative customers, and instead, allocates three of average ability, accepting that the final customer rating will be unchanged.
- **Option 4** – Jane allocates her three weakest accountants, risking the client's fury and the possible end of the relationship.

If you were Jane what would you do?

Let's take a look at the knock-on effects of each of these options:

- **Option 1** – Decline the client's invitation to conduct the audit – loss of revenue and earnings – bad.
- **Option 2** – Jane to complete the audit personally with two assistants – Jane's time to manage the relationships with other clients and her team members decreases significantly for several weeks – temporarily bad.
- **Option 3** – Jane mentally categorizes the client as "difficult", retains her best three accountants for more appreciative customers, and instead, allocates three of average ability, accepting that the final customer rating will be unchanged – accepts the status quo and declines the possibility of higher performance levels.

Which means that the only viable option with a possible upside is:

- **Option 4** – Jane allocates her three weakest accountants, risking the client's fury and the possible ending of the relationship.

How could there be an upside for this seemingly obvious wrong choice? Well, by working with a really tough customer, the weakest accountants might learn more and gain in self-confidence. That in turn could raise the average ability of the team. And on balance, Jane may decide that the possible upside of team development is greater than the possible downside of contract termination. Of course, the more likely outcome will be a higher level of customer dissatisfaction and the possible ending of the relationship. Bad.

So, after examining these alternatives, Jane will probably decide to stick with the original and obvious decision, i.e. choose the three accountants with the highest ability and incentivize them to achieve the best ever customer satisfaction rating.

This is Jane's moment of power. Carefully thought through and exercized. As I said before, job done!

Want to know the final outcome? I told you it was a true story. Go to Chapter 9 and learn how this manager was able to achieve a brilliant result for all the wrong reasons!

This simple example contains much for a manager to think about. Many more examples and typical work situations are described in the following chapters. But every example will have the same objective – to improve your self-awareness and self-confidence as a manager and, through that, self-improvement to greater team success as well.

Moment of Power – Example 2

"People don't work the same way as they used to."

Joanna leads a team of eight "Generation Y" people, who she allows to work at times which are convenient to the individuals. Some come in early and leave early, others arrive late and leave late. They all put in a good shift, but her peers who lead comparable teams are more conventional and see her tolerance and flexibility as disruptive and are urging you, the boss, to insist that all teams start and finish at the same time. Output is similar between the teams.

This example is about the boss being prepared to think differently in order to increase total team performance. It was Stephen Covey who coined the phrase – "How you see the problem is the problem" and it may apply in this situation too. The sub-managers have different styles. Some observers would see Joanna as more enlightened, more aware of the needs of GenY people, whereas her colleagues may be more old school. Other observers might see the opposite: Joanna as being too tolerant, less of a manager perhaps; better to let people know where they stand, insist on conformance to standards. For the top boss – is the "problem" with Joanna, with her co-managers, or neither?

The moment of power? When the manager doesn't rush to make a judgement, but instead examines closely the output data and performance of each of the sub-teams and when he or she challenges all of the sub-managers to explain why they think that their way is best. The overall boss's personal preferences should remain undeclared while he or she insists that if team output and performance is paramount, then personal prejudices should be subordinated. Everyone involved should be encouraged to think differently. This is the type of data that should be discussed for each of the teams involved:

- Output volume, output volume per employee.
- Output cost, output cost per employee.
- Quality standard, number of faults/returns.
- Employee engagement/job satisfaction ratings.
- Supply team ratings.
- Customer team ratings.
- Staff turnover.

If there is no discernible difference between the teams, why change anything?

But there may be another moment of power lying right beneath the surface. I would urge the boss to swap the sub-managers and let Joanna manage a different team with her flexible approach, and let one of her peers take over her old team and insist on the same start and finish times. Whilst watching output performance closely, of course, the boss should re-evaluate after a few months or a much shorter time to see if big differences occur. I bet the new data will reveal the most effective management style for each of the teams.

So instead of having sub-managers with "It's my way or the highway" attitudes, you will have created managers that have come to realize that their focus must be on the ultimate objectives of customer satisfaction, production and productivity. Of course, the boss may learn also that one or more of his sub-managers may lack the confidence, personal security or ability to manage the team in a way that does not totally align with their own personal preferences, and that may impact future moments of power when filling job vacancies.

Moment of Power – Example 3:

"With me, what you see is what you get!"

But you're told that there is widespread criticism of you and your management style being circulated on Facebook.

Is your first reaction a negative, "Oh no!" or is it a positive, "Great! What an opportunity!"? Be honest. The moment of power? Three options:

- **Option 1** – Ignore the criticism.
- **Option 2** – Retaliate.
- **Option 3** – Socialize your awareness and knowledge of the criticism with a statement that you wish to address the

issues giving rise to the comments, and call a meeting in two or three days' time so that everyone gets a chance to think about what they will say.

"Can I have everyone's attention for a moment please? It has been brought to my notice that there is widespread criticism being circulated of myself and my style of working, including comments on Facebook. I want to address the issues that have given rise to these comments and make everyone aware of the background to the actions I have taken. I will arrange for a team meeting in a few days' time and want everyone to feel free to express their true feelings. Some of you may be reluctant to say what you really feel, so I will arrange for an independent person to act as go-between. Thank you."

Moment of power? When the manager decides to confront the brutal, wounding truth with the aim of addressing the underlying issues that have given rise to the criticism.

So, I urge you to explore the moments of power which are described and illustrated with real-life examples throughout the book, so that you know where to look when the need arises.

It may be possible to arrange a private and confidential talk with one of the authors if you are grappling with an awkward or challenging problem at work. When you need input or an exchange of ideas on how to approach your situation, or if you would simply like to share an example or two from your own personal experiences, please email: johncross@moments-of-power.com. Until such a time, enjoy this book and all the insights into managing it contains.

Part One

Your Rewarding Job

YOUR RESPONSIBILITIES

1.1   Ignore your job description

This book is designed to make you a better manager. In order for you to realize and acknowledge your progress we need to establish a measurement guideline. So, I'm going to start with a question, and you may wish to seek the views of others before deciding on your answer.

I'd like you to think of the combined performance of you and your team over the past six months and imagine that everything has gone perfectly – you have all the right people, their work is perfect, you've improved productivity and set new standards for interfacing with other teams and departments. Recognition, awards and money have flowed freely in your direction. That may be a bit of a stretch of course, but bear with me. I'd like you to give that imaginary performance a mark of 100%.

Now think about your actual situation and performance over the past six months and give you and your team a combined estimated score by comparison. Enter it here .... %.

I have asked this question many times of thousands of real managers over the past 13 years in my day job and the actual marks have varied between 10% and 95%, averaging about 65%. This means that every manager I have met has indicated the potential for improvement. Fantastic.

Why have I asked you this question? Because now, and maybe for the first time, I'm going to tell you your real job:

> Your job is to increase that mark by 1%, and as soon as you have achieved it, by the next 1%.

Don't be too disappointed if the mark drops from time to time because of extraneous factors or indeed, your own mismanagement – just work on the extra 1%.

Forget about your job description[1] (even if you are one of the lucky(?) ones to have one), unless, of course, it says exactly that.

But how, I hear you ask, am I to generate that extra 1%?

Start by asking this simple question: What will you do tomorrow to inspire individuals to greater job and personal satisfaction and the entire team to work together more efficiently? Because that is what this book is all about. Moments of power which either have the potential to contribute to the extra 1%, or the power to reduce it. Even if you disagree with half of the examples, the other half may help you to enjoy your job a little more.

There are two other jobs you have: the first is to get the same jobs done to the same or better standards with fewer resources and smaller budgets and the second is to make yourself redundant. Making yourself redundant means that the team or your organization don't need your skills or even an actual person in that role any longer. But not to worry, there are greater challenges for you if you want them.

To summarize your real job:

- Increase team output in increments of 1%.
- Get the same jobs done to the same or better standards with fewer resources and smaller budgets.
- Make yourself redundant.

1.2 Embrace your role as a soccer coach and an orchestra conductor

You might not realize it, but you are a unique combination of your day job, a soccer coach and an orchestra conductor! As a manager, you have one of the most challenging but most rewarding jobs in the whole world! Congratulations!

You want me to explain? OK.

Let's start with the soccer manager. A soccer coach knows the talents, skills and mindsets of each and every one of his entire squad at any one time. For the next game, the coach assesses the strengths and weaknesses of the team's opponents and selects the 11 players best suited to overcome and exploit them respectively. At the pre-match briefing, the coach outlines the roles and responsibilities of each of the players so that everyone knows their position on the pitch and what they have to do; because they also know the positions of their colleagues and their roles and responsibilities, they know where and how they fit into the overall game plan.

The game kicks off but, after a little while, the coach notices that his game plan is not working as intended and he makes some changes to the organization of the team, making a substitution. He starts off with a plan, fully aware that it may not survive the first 15 minutes.

Now think of the parallels with your job as a manager. What is your game plan for the next day or week? Knowing the talents, skills and mindsets of each of your people, ask yourself whether they are all aware of the tasks ahead and the part they will individually play in the collective team effort? A day or two later, equivalent to the 15 minutes on the soccer pitch, one of your team becomes sick. If you have a substitute great, but if not, then how will you adjust the roles and responsibilities of the remaining members to get the jobs done on time? So, the next time you watch a soccer match on the television, concentrate on the manager more than the players and ask yourself whether you watch the performances of your team with the same focus and concentration. Enjoy the game!

Now let's examine your role as an orchestra conductor. Like the soccer coach, you are acutely aware of the talents, skills and mindsets of the entire orchestra. The strength of the string, brass, woodwind and percussion sections and the balance between them reflects the venue, the occasion and the concert music selected. The team is ready to go. The audience settles into their seats and you raise your baton. Why? To keep the different sections in time with each other. Without the conductor, the cellos may not know precisely when to come in because the sound from the violins takes time to travel across the stage. If the cellos waited until they heard their cue then they would be too late. The discordant result would encourage people to leave the auditorium fairly quickly.[2]

In your job as a manager, you have to make sure that the work of one of your people isn't holding up another member of your team, nor accelerating away from them. It is your job to coordinate the work between the individual members of your team, so that the optimum combined performance is achieved consistently. So, the next time you watch a concert, concentrate on the conductor more than the musicians and ask yourself whether you coordinate the work of your people with the same precision and encouragement.[3]

A footnote on the question of mindsets. You may have the equivalent of a uniquely gifted player or musician in your group, but they are unlikely to contribute much if their mindset is not right. They may be distracted or preoccupied by something either at work or at home. Either way, you will need to decide if their lack of focus warrants a relegation to the substitutes' bench for the time being, and explain why, confidentially of course.

> ### *Your* Moment of Power
>
> When you respond quickly to changes in circumstances and adjust working hours and individual work allocations to achieve the maximum possible team output for the period.

1.3   Focus on customer satisfaction

All of your objectives and those of your people need to contribute to one or more of only three top-level goals:

For commercial organizations:

- Customer satisfaction.
- Margin.
- Market share.

For not-for-profit and government organizations:

- Customer satisfaction.
- Delivery.
- Stakeholder engagement.

Make sure that your team understand where their individual little projects will have a positive effect; let them see and understand the contribution they are making to the big picture. Improving customer satisfaction should be the number one goal for any organization, and it's the most challenging. Satisfied clients become an organization's advocates, spreading words about you to a wider audience and, with social media, the speed of spread can be lightning fast. Pleased with your service or product, increased sales feed market share and improved market share contains the promise of higher margins.

You might not have an external customer on whom to focus, in which case you should aim to understand the "products" or "services" that you offer to other teams both inside and outside of your own organization.

Take these two contrasting examples from personal experience:

I bought a coat from Land's End for about £80. After about 18 months, the front zip fastener broke. I telephoned the company to order a replacement, expecting to spend another £80. "Oh no sir," said the sales assistant, "our products have a lifetime guarantee, so I'll send you another one together with a freepost label for the return of the faulty one." The new one duly arrived and the old one was easily returned. Excellent service – very pleased. Then I received a telephone call. "Sir, the price of the replacement item is lower, £50, and we have tried to refund the difference to you, but we have what must be an expired card number on file. Could you give me your current card number please and we'll credit £30 to you?" How brilliant! I'm now their advocate – SHOP AT LAND'S END!

But with my mobile phone service provider, O_2, the story is different. Having identified the new handset that I wanted, I contacted O_2 directly and asked for their best deal. I then compared it to the offers from O_2's retail partners and was surprised to find that I could get the same or even better deals from their partners instead. You will understand my disappointment that after 13 years with the same company, they treat me as if I were a new subscriber. Loyalty, it seems, only appears to work one way.

Your Moment of Power

When your explanations to staff about their role in achieving the "bigger picture" create enthusiasm and gain their commitment.

2

YOUR GOALS

2.1 Let your people set their own objectives

Many managers think that it's their responsibility to set objectives for their people.[1] That's what happens in the overwhelming majority of cases. But if *you* allocate them, they are *your* objectives, not *theirs*. If your people fail to reach them for whatever reason, some might be tempted to say, "I always thought that was impossible", and their commitment to them may be weak. But, if you agree to their suggestions, even if they are not perfect, their ownership of them will be much stronger and they are much more likely to achieve them.

Open an early discussion with each of your people with this phrase:

> *"We need to set two or three objectives for you for the next month (quarter or financial year), please let me have your thoughts on what these might be for the following two or three areas."*

Shorter-term objectives should feed into the longer-term ones.

Objectives keep everyone thinking about what they need to do, and thinking about their output and contribution tends to improve productivity.

But when agreeing objectives, remember the acronym, SMART: Specific, Measurable, Achievable, Realistic and Time specific.

Make sure that only one person has the responsibility of achieving a particular goal, even though others may be involved in its achievement. Never divide responsibility, thus avoiding people saying "Sorry, I thought you (they) were doing that."

Once you have agreed the objectives verbally, ask your staff member to put them in writing to you, not you to them, and ask them to include any necessary timescales and/or milestones if appropriate. You can then top and tail it before returning it within 24–48 hours.

Having agreed on the objective, then request their plan of how they will accomplish it in writing (one side of A4 only), but give them a little time to really think about their challenge. They may need to clarify their understanding or ask questions.

Review progress with your colleagues formally and regularly.

Your Moment of Power

When you allow your people to influence and shape their objectives and resist setting them unilaterally.

2.2   Try not to set targets

You can forget about quick double-digit improvements to performance – life just isn't like that. It is actually built on slow, as opposed to quick, fixes.[2] The extraordinarily successful British Olympic cycling team employ a manager of marginal gains. Tiny advances, which in themselves don't mean much until they are combined with all of the other tiny gains.

I once asked the managing director of a clothing firm who had achieved spectacular success, with 30% – 40% year-on-year growth over many years, how he had targeted this performance. His reply impressed me. "We don't set revenue or sales targets, John; instead we provide accurate, up-to-the-minute internal and external operational data at everyone's fingertips, and we empower the people to act upon that data quickly. Our people take pride in driving the business forward and we reward them well. Targets may have actually restricted our growth."

Do your people have all of the real-time operational data they need to do their job? Are the electronic links available and robust?

Success is defined by many organizations as hitting targets, and I've always found this management discipline difficult. Normally targets are for the financial year, but as we know, a lot can, and does, change within that time frame. So what is the value of an arbitrary goal for 31 December or 31 March, probably set about 13–15 months previously? I don't know.

It is not possible to set the right target for next year. Why? Because you cannot allow or plan for the "unknown unknowns" as Donald Rumsfeld put it. Yes, you can aim for an extra 10% of whatever for next year, but does it mean that everyone has failed if you only achieve 8%? Hitting 10% early may restrict effort to do even better if the rewards are not strongly promoted or visible. So what purpose do targets serve? People have a tendency to become obsessive about them, they dominate conversations and they direct attention inwards and away from the ever-changing needs of the end user or internal customer.

It has been reported that some managers in the UK's wonderful National Health Service became so preoccupied with hitting targets that their primary responsibility of patient care was seriously neglected – to such as extent that, in some hospitals, patients died needlessly. Unbelievable!

Indeed, so powerful do these targets become in the minds of a very small minority of people that they will manipulate, massage or simply falsify the figures in order to claim victory. I have known managers who have instructed their teams to sign up customers at the end of one financial year because of the promise to the client that they could cancel without penalty early in the following financial year. I have known good men and women who have resigned from their jobs when asked to falsify the numbers.

Your Moment of Power

When you don't mindlessly obsess about targets. Do right by your internal or end-user customer and success will follow.

2.3 Identify performance potential

Maximizing output is your aim, the extra 1%. But maximum output potential will vary during the year because of any number of external forces. With a competitor in trouble with reliability, maybe your maximum potential for this quarter is double the previous quarter's output? The following quarter may see the maximum potential reduced by 60% because volcanic ash in the troposphere restricts airline transportation. How will you identify and then cope with such unpredictable variations in potential? How will you ramp up production to exploit a doubling of demand? And then in the following quarter cut back dramatically?[3]

Obviously these would be extreme circumstances and apply to an externally focused team. But how would the same principle apply in reality to an accounts department or health and safety team, where such seismic changes are unlikely? After all, they have targets too, don't they?

If you are worried about adhering to this principle for internal units, return to "output potential" not workload. A finance team know that there are times of the month when they are busier than other times. They cope with busy, perhaps indicating to their manager a performance close to their "output potential". The busy period subsides. So does output. At this point, an effective finance manager may consider deploying the skills of his or her team outside of the department, explaining the intricacies of a treasury function to the uninitiated in other departments. The accounts team has the "output potential", but is the manager exploiting it?

And "output potential" is equally relevant on a personal level. Once I joined a large UK company and met a number of my future colleagues on the induction programme. As we got to know one another better, we exchanged brief career histories and why each of us had been persuaded to join this particular company.

One such person was Keith, who proudly told me that he "had been offered every job that he had ever applied for" and was quickly dismayed when I told him I was sorry to hear it. Asked to explain, I told him that he had never established his most rewarding potential employment threshold. Only by failing to secure several positions could he gradually come to realize at what level he would be best suited, because doing a job that does not require you to use your talents fully is not fulfilling, but neither is a job which demands a level of skill that you don't possess. Because he had never failed, he could have been operating well below his potential.

You might be familiar with the acronym, PESTLE. It represents those external forces whose interaction will largely determine your team's demand or output potential: Political, Economic, Sociological, Technological, Legislative and Environmental. It is a complementary analysis to SWOT: Strengths, Weaknesses, Opportunities and Threats. Both models should be completed regularly and then acted upon. You could even do a PESTLE and SWOT analysis on yourself!

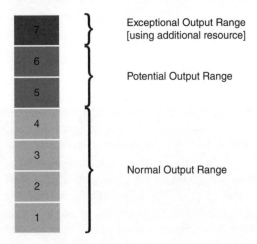

Where would you place last months output?

Figure 2.1

Your Moment of Power

When you identify and communicate your view of the output potential for the next period and then reorganize resources to deliver it.

YOUR PERFORMANCE

3.1 Have up-to-date performance statistics at your fingertips

Do you deliver what your "customers" expect from you and your team? Some departments have external "customers" (i.e. sales, accounts payable, complaints, regulatory etc.) and others have internal ones. Do you meet with them or their representatives regularly and discuss your team's outputs?

Figure 3.1 below illustrates three data collection points for you to study regularly. Box 1 statistics show a number of different metrics on inputs from your supplier team. Box 2 statistics show your own measurements and calculations on both your process and your outputs. Box 3 statistics show the data that you receive from your "customer" team, which should match your Box 2 data.

Box 4 contains suggestions for the type of records that you could chart regularly and share with your team. Knowing the detail of your team's performance means it can then be compared with other teams both internally and externally to highlight key operational differences, and this will be essential if you need more resources.

Do the statistics reveal areas that need improvement? What are the options for achieving that improvement? Are investments in new hardware or software required? Collect as many statistics

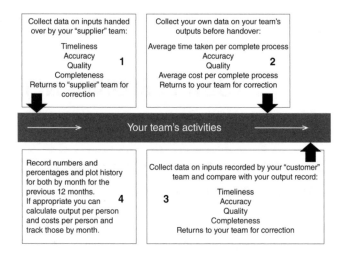

| Collect data on inputs handed over by your "supplier" team:

Timeliness
Accuracy
Quality **1**
Completeness
Returns to "supplier" team for correction | Collect your own data on your team's outputs before handover:

Average time taken per complete process
Accuracy
Quality **2**
Average cost per complete process
Returns to your team for correction |

Your team's activities

| Record numbers and percentages and plot history for both by month for the previous 12 months.
If appropriate you can **4** calculate output per person and costs per person and track those by month. | Collect data on inputs recorded by your "customer" team and compare with your output record:

3 Timeliness
Accuracy
Quality
Completeness
Returns to your team for correction |

Figure 3.1

as you can, from as many angles as you can. The more you know, the more informed will be your decision making.

The model above works for any team, in every industry, as well as not-for-profit organizations and government departments. Over many years, I have often been surprised that senior sales people, from a variety of different companies, could not tell me how many products or services were sold by their company in the previous year; or how many projects went live, or how many projects were delivered on time, to budget and to specification. These details are essential for all client discussions.

What does your model look like?

When you have it complete, you may consider checking to see whether the data adheres to the Pareto principle[1], or the 80/20[2] rule as it more often known.

For example, 80% of your sales revenue will probably come from the top 20% of your customers by volume; 80% of your sales will probably come from 20% of your sales people; 80% of your problems will probably come from 20% of your products or services.

The Pareto principle can prove valuable when prioritizing your efforts.

Your Moment of Power

When you demonstrate control and understanding by dropping up-to-date performance statistics into conversations regularly.

3.2 Draw an activity tree

A useful way of understanding how the outputs of your team are achieved, is to create an activity tree[3] (see Figure 3.2 below). This method breaks down the various stages of work into discrete components, which can be examined separately to increase speed and/or reduce cost. Amazingly, as simple as this may appear, I have found many examples of activities over the years that, when put under a management microscope, do not need to be done at all. Like many of the recommendations given for you throughout this book, you don't need to do it personally – delegate it, but allow enough time for it to be completed properly.

In fact, why not get the whole team involved in a detailed examination of each activity to see where efficiencies may be achieved. It's worth looking at the following in detail:

- Average time taken for each activity.
- Skills required for each activity.

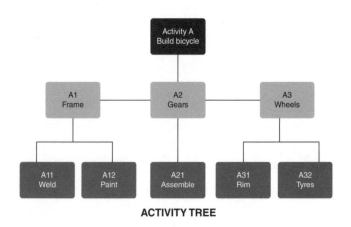

ACTIVITY TREE

Figure 3.2

- Resources required at each stage.
- Cost of those resources.
- Total elapsed time at the completion of each sequential stage.
- Average cost for the completion of each activity (more difficult than it would at first appear, and help from your finance people is normally required).
- Total cost of all activities.
- On which activities is 80% of the time required.
- On which activities is 80% of the cost incurred.

Does the potential for the extra 1% in performance lie here?

Your Moment of Power

When you break down your team's activities into easily understood components and conduct or commission a detailed examination of them for efficiency savings.

3.3 Don't shy away from making or recommending big investments

In the first chapter, I stated that one of the three main jobs of a manager is to "Get the same jobs done to the same or better standards with fewer resources and smaller budgets", and the previous section described the activity tree model to help you identify options for further examination.

Be careful when thinking about better ways of doing things that you do not become obsessed with cutting costs and forget about the big investments that are often required to change the dynamic or model of your work.[4] Henry Ford may have tried to make horses go faster at first, but his real success came when he created a novel way to move people around the planet.

Sometimes it takes a significant amount of money and many years to make a process more efficient. Don't shy away from being the first person to move towards a different way of doing things. It can certainly be more inspiring for your people to be involved in a programme which is attempting a paradigm shift. Take for example the original workers at PARC – the Palo Alto Research Centre set up by Xerox to come up with the "office of the future" in the mid-1970s. That original team pioneered almost every office innovation in use today (i.e. personal computer, tablets, mouse, keyboard, the GUI interface, laser printers, etc.). Xerox thought it unwise to set about changing over to a paperless office and left these inventions to be harnessed by others, but the point remains, it took time and money to generate the future!

Encourage ideas for improvement at every opportunity.

Consider the use of the following hardware and software developments:

- Mobile/tablet based computing.
- Cloud-based storage and processing.
- Robotics.
- Agile software development.
- Nano-technology.
- Social media and collaboration tools.
- Software as a Service (SAAS).
- APIs (Application Programming Interfaces).

Finally, a question: What material are you reading regularly to maintain your currency with new information systems and technological developments? Or do you have friends and colleagues who can keep you up to speed?

Try www.theregister.co.uk.

Your Moment of Power

When you spot a new technology or development which may contain the potential to improve your world.

3.4　Prepare for the possibility that every action you take, may inadvertently create an equal and opposite reaction

Forgive me for making a slight adjustment and expansion to Newton's Third Law, but discuss with others the possible reactions to your planned initiatives before you communicate them to a wider audience. By attempting to solve one issue, you may inadvertently create another where none existed before. Let me give you an example from the world of health care.

From the authorities in the UK a new national diktat arrived – "Everyone arriving at the Accident and Emergency departments must be seen within four hours." Seems OK on first consideration, so where could the equal and opposite reaction be? In responding to the new diktat, managers ask – "When does the clock start?" Answer – "When patients arrive in the A & E department." So patients are now left in the ambulances outside, tying up valuable resources and putting the lives of others who need an ambulance in jeopardy. Yes – patients are seen in four hours once they enter the department, but they could have spent another hour or two outside on a trolley. Not what the original objective tried to achieve.

This concept is also known as the law of unintended causes and has a large and long history in the social sciences.[5]

For your own plans and changes, it will be better to ask for input from others:

> *"Please look at these plans carefully and try to identify adverse knock-on effects that I may not have foreseen. I may have to change the plans if they cause unintended negative consequences."*

But what about the new initiatives that are handed down from on high? The responsibility to signal possible opposite reactions rests with you!

For every action there is an equal and opposite reaction. I bet there is evidence of this law in your organization, right now.

Your Moment of Power

When you seek input in order to highlight possible adverse knock-on effects brought about by new initiatives in order that they may be mitigated.

YOUR MESSAGES

4.1   Create sticky headline messages

In many parts of Africa, educating the general public about AIDS and its prevention involves groups of travelling actors performing an attention-grabbing play which vividly demonstrates the dangers of unprotected sex. Pure theatre. They don't use historical facts and figures, but instead tell a story about a teenager just like those in the audience, and the consequences that they face after making the wrong choices. Delivering a message without MS PowerPoint, whiteboards or overhead projectors. Imagine that!

I suspect that a lot of your people will have difficulty remembering your team's vision, mission, strategy and objectives. Why? Because they are expressed and articulated in unemotional corporate communications or management speak. You need goals that are achievable, memorable, exciting and worthy, but above all, they should be understood and embraced at an emotional level.

Managers have a huge responsibility to paint the team's tasks in vivid terms which connect with the humanity and feelings of each individual of the team.[1] Forget the "management speak"; instead construct a story or parable which grips your team's attention and energizes and motivates them. Stories with sticky headlines

The 5-Minute Suitcase

The 24-Hour
Packet of Crisps

Figure 4.1
Frito-Lay image CNBC089 reproduced by kind permission of Frito-Lay

can endure over long periods. Repeat them often, because repetition is key to making things "stick" in the minds of your audience.

Two examples. One airline developed "The 5-Minute Suitcase" as a clear and unambiguous strategy to improve customer satisfaction, meaning that baggage was transferred from the hold to the collection carousel in less than five minutes from engine shutdown. The second example was called "The 24-Hour Packet of Crisps", or in the US, "The 24-Hour Packet of Potato Chips". This food manufacturer decided to use freshness as a competitive weapon and embarked upon a 12-month programme to reduce the time from when the product left the baking ovens to reaching the supermarkets' shelves to less than 24 hours.

Both examples took a long time to achieve and cost a lot of money, but everyone working on those two projects knew precisely what the goal was, and they identified with it as a worthwhile goal. They knew the part they had to play and committed to it at an emotional level. They felt that they were doing good.

So, ask yourself whether the way that your goals are expressed have as strong an emotional pull to do good as "The 5-Minute Suitcase" or "The 24-Hour Packet of Crisps"?

Your Moment of Power

When you devise and promote your own powerful story headline to challenge the status quo.

4.2   Change behaviours

Effective leaders tackle the most challenging work. Work that requires fundamental change in the behaviour of the followers. Sounds a bit grand doesn't it? And it sounds very difficult. But think of it like this – only an effective leader can swing an organization away from its focus on technology and get it to accept the customer as the driving force; only an effective leader can ask communities to accept compromise with opposing ideologies and, much closer to home, only an effective leader can ask people to accept significant changes in work practices. The important word in the preceding explanation is "accept".

Many ineffective leaders make changes which are not accepted; many ineffective leaders fail at every given opportunity to convince their followers of the "rightness" of the proposed course of action.

In situations where ineffective leaders make changes by diktat instead of persuasion, followers react in different ways. What happens when an ineffective leader orders compliance with a new operating standard? Potential chaos, because some will make the change, some will continue to follow the "old" method, some will use neither method, and some will use both methods. Then instead of only one way of operating, there will be four.

An effective leader will consider "burning the bridges" so that the followers will not be tempted to access and return to the "old" system.

If you and your team work in an office, there will be those who are the "early adopters" of the new system and those who we can classify as "late adopters". At this point you may consider making changes to seating positions so that an "early" sits next to a "late". It is quite normal for the "late" to be accelerated through the change by a closer socialization with the "early".

Spend much more time with those who are prepared to change easily and quickly and find ways of promoting their early achievements to the wider group:

> "John has accepted the changes without too much fuss and is getting on OK with them. It's difficult to change habits of a lifetime, but I know it's going to be OK."

And don't be in too much of a rush. Listen to the reactions of your people and, seek out levels of resistance. They may indicate that a small adjustment to your new plan is warranted and may even improve it!

But before asking others to change their behaviour, look in the mirror. What behaviours in yourself do you want or need to change to move closer towards the extra 1%? Only when you've made the change can you ask others to change. You need to set the example!

This is a point which UK politicians almost universally fail to acknowledge. For example, how can they ask government employees to take a smaller pension when they don't?[2]

Your Moment of Power

When you focus your time and energy on the people who will be first to change, because they in turn will change others in your absence.

4.3 Don't underestimate the costs or timescales of any changes

If the workload of your team is increasing, you may need more staff, more workspace and new software. Your boss asks for the likely costs. Now, is the time to look back at previous projects in your organization and, with help from your finance people, estimate the time and cost overruns on the last dozen or so initiatives and then apply the average percentage overrun to your final estimates. Why? Because you're demonstrating a thoroughness and worldly recognition that most projects fail on one or more of the following parameters: specification, time and budget.[3]

This may appear to be a simple task, but many organizations don't follow up on completed projects and compare the actual figures with those forecast at the beginning. So, if previous history is unavailable, make all of the detailed calculations that you can, remembering to include internal costs such as retraining time, and then double the final figure. If you work in the public sector (and you are dealing with greater accountability and layers of bureaucracy) then multiply the total by a factor between three and five.

With the Olympics being staged every four years, you would think that the organizers of London 2012 would have been able to produce a reasonably close initial estimate. No, the original quotation in 2005 was for £2.4bn, however the final bill stood at £8.92bn, nearly four times the original estimate.

The trouble with spreadsheets is that they produce precise figures down to the nearest dollar or euro. But when presenting or explaining your estimates, you don't need to be so precise. Use a range and give yourself plenty of leeway.

"I believe the final costs will be in the range of £10–13k."

You may be tempted to ignore this advice and go for the smallest amount you can get away with in order to get the go-ahead from on high. Perfectly understandable, but the risk is that you may need to go back and ask for more time and/or money, perhaps more than once. Reputation damaged.

Senior executives know, usually from the bitter experience of past failures, that things don't work out the way they were intended. So be pragmatic, argue for the padding and be open with your reasons. Then come in under budget. Reputation enhanced.

Your Moment of Power

When you show bosses that you have done your home-work on previous projects and as a result, estimate costs and timescales with worldly experience.

4.4   Do good

Not only do companies need to make a minimum level of profit to prosper, it is widely accepted that they should also do good for society at large. Individuals should have a personal responsibility to make a contribution towards some larger social goal. Fortunately, many organizations and individuals do so.

So, does your team make a contribution towards some larger social goal? It could bring benefits to your local community, the local environment, or advance science for the benefit of the human race. Your team should do good.

Finding a purposeful and worthwhile social goal could be the secret to securing greater commitment to team harmony and therefore output. If you haven't done so already, why not discuss this whole area with your team and develop some options to consider carefully?

> "Ladies and Gentlemen, I would like us all to think of something that we could do together to help others. Please think of one or two initiatives that you would support, and we can discuss them at our next team meeting."

First of all, look at what talents you have in your team. Someone may be a good artist or musician. Another may speak a foreign language and another may play in a local football team. Armed with the knowledge of the talents in your team, you may consider where the group's interests lie and what you want to achieve collectively. Here are some examples for you and your team to consider:

- Supporting an agreed charity or two over the long term by holding regular events and promotions.
- Supporting an art project, festival or museum.
- Supporting local artists, musicians or sportsmen and women.

- Supporting a local school, perhaps by explaining how your organization works and devising a business game for the teenagers.
- Supporting a local youth club.
- Supporting a green issue or an animal welfare project.
- Looking at what your company throws away and finding a better home for the material at home or overseas.
- Recycling.

Adopt a project that will take a lot of time and effort to achieve. Perhaps a year or two, and mainly in your own time, not the company's. Try to build something that will last for the long term and continue after you have left the team.

Chances are that many of your people already support a charity or lend a hand at various social functions. Find out what these social contributions are and get behind them. You're almost on your way!

Your Moment of Power

When you and your team volunteer to do something for others who need some help, without benefitting from it either personally or professionally.

Part Two

It's All About You

YOUR FOCUS

5.1 Inspire them!

Your roles as a manager and as a leader are primarily about inspiration. A manager should inspire each person individually with something that connects with their personality and work–life demands; whereas a leader should inspire the whole team by developing and communicating a sense of community and a worthwhile goal.

Marcus Buckingham and Curt Coffman offer a supporting and brilliant explanation of the difference between the duties of a manager and the duties of a leader in their book *First Break All The Rules*[1]:

> *"Great managers know and value the unique abilities and even the eccentricities of their employees, and they learn how best to integrate them into a coordinated plan of attack.*
>
> *This is the exact opposite of what great leaders do.*
>
> *Great leaders discover what is universal and capitalize on it. Their job is to rally people toward a better future. Leaders can succeed in this only when they can cut through differences of race, sex, age, nationality and personality and, using stories and celebrating heroes, tap into those very few needs we all share."*

So, how do you score yourself on the management/leadership spectrum?

First, think about the best manager you know or have known. It may be someone you have worked for or who has managed another team that has been close to you.

The best manager I have known is ....

Score 100%

By comparison with the person named above, I would give myself this score as a manager:

Score .... %

Next, think of who is the best leader you know or have known. It may be someone you have worked for or who has led another team or department. Someone who has inspired their followers.

The best leader I have known is ....

Score 100%

By comparison with the person named above, I would give myself this score as a leader:

Score .... %

And finally, list the three main steps that you want to take to make yourself a more effective leader and manager:

Action & Planned Timescale (e.g., read the biography of Winston Churchill or attend a business school programme or...)	Completed
1	
2	
3	

Your Moment of Power

When you accept, genuinely and seriously, that you can do better and accept the challenge.

5.2 Spend more time managing, less time operating

If you think of a typical period (quarter, half year etc.), what percentage of your time do you spend *operating* (doing things) and what percentage do you spend *managing* (thinking about your job as a manager and implementing those initiatives and little touches that can improve the well-being and productivity of each of your people)?

Think about it like this. You're a lumberjack – an operator of a chainsaw that all day, cuts down trees; that's *operating*.

By comparison, if you are managing the forests, you regularly climb into your helicopter to view where to deploy your lumberjacks; you assess the area they have cleared or replanted (have you hit the milestones?) and the areas remaining (will you hit the final deadline/target?); do you need more or fewer lumberjacks; with the seasons changing do you need to change their working hours/pay/retainer; do you have enough back-up components or spare chainsaws in case of some malfunction; is there an emergency procedure and medical help if one of your lumberjacks cuts their own leg off? And when needs must, you have to fill in as an extra lumberjack as well, or use your vast experience when a difficult felling is required. That's *managing*!

When asked this question in my day job I get answers ranging from 20% operating/80% managing to 95% operating/5% managing. Both are probably a little skewed from what I perceive to be the ideal balance of about 50/50 over time. But there will be days when you spend all of your time managing, or all of your time operating. Remember to compensate, but try for at least 15 minutes every day to reflect upon what you and the team are producing, i.e., are you progressing towards the extra 1%?

While by no means an exhaustive list, let's examine a few examples of what I consider to be managing:

Action	Managing
Digging deep to understand the motivations of the individuals on your team and thinking of different options to leverage them in the workplace.	✓
Sensing or determining the maximum output level of each individual and trying out ways of getting their performance up to that level consistently throughout every day.	✓
Sensing or determining the morale or team spirit of your team and trying out ways of improving it even further.	✓
Looking at the activities of your team in detail and trying out ways of reaching the objectives with less resource.	✓
Determining output potential for the next periods.	✓
Improving the coordination of tasks between your team members.	✓
Praising and admonishing, perhaps even daily.	✓
Maintaining and reinforcing your personal and corporate standards.	✓
Recruiting new team members with the right character.	✓
Identifying possible future problems and devising ways of mitigating their effect.	✓
Thinking of ways to increase output by 1% every day.	✓
Maintaining a positive, upbeat demeanour and a fun work atmosphere.	✓
Asking searching questions.	✓
Communicating progress with compelling visual imagery.	✓

And a few examples of operating (but often mistakenly thought to be managing):

Action	Managing
Becoming focused on the work of one or two individuals to the exclusion of others for more than one hour.	✗
Filling in to help your team members with their work for more than one hour.	✗
Doing the same or similar work as your team members for more than one hour.	✗

Regardless of the role (managing or operating), always be purposeful when you engage with your people. One of the biggest threats to your team's motivation and enjoyment comes when you personally have little operational work to do – and you decide to go walkabout, interrupt, check progress, add a bit of what you think is value (but rarely is), talk about last night's sports game or the latest film.

So, even if a little time creeps into your schedule, don't distract your team members by engaging in the above behaviour. Instead, let the individuals on your team make progress towards the goals they may have set themselves for the day, free from mindless interruption.

Now, reflect upon the past and then look ahead for the next few months. What split between operating and managing do you think is right for your circumstances and challenges?

	Past	
	Operating %	Managing %

Last Month

Last Quarter

Last Year

	Future	
	Operating %	Managing %

Next Month

Next Quarter

Next Year

Next, consider the risks to your future model. Who and what could divert you from becoming a more effective manager? I've included a few reasons below, but add more for your own circumstances.

Risk	Risk Priority High, Moderate, Low
New boss needs more of my time.	
Loss of one team member, need to recruit replacement.	
Departmental reorganization. Team integrated with another.	
Workload increases, need to do more operating.	
Staff absent for sickness/training/maternity leave etc.	

Your Moment of Power

When you decide to monitor and record the percentage of time each week that you spend operating, and introduce changes so that you can spend more time managing and less time operating.

5.3 Focus on your strengths, don't dwell on your weaknesses

All too often an appraisal by your boss focuses not on what you're good at, but on what you need to improve upon. Your so-called development plan.

Is this really a good idea? Let's find out by taking this line of thinking onto the sports field and imagine David Beckham in training. He's exceptional at crossing the ball with pinpoint accuracy from the right wing of the football (or soccer) pitch. It's his key strength. However, he's not so good at running back and tackling the opposition for the ball. What does he practise every moment in training – yes – crossing the ball with his right foot.

So what do you regard as your key strength? Let us suppose that you and your colleagues agree on what it is and your score is 9 out of 10. Fantastic! Many people would feel good about this and then look at their weaknesses and try and improve one or two of them. Don't. Instead, examine and decide how you could achieve a score of 9.1 and then 9.2.

How could you increase an already high score? To achieve 9 out of 10, your assessors regard you as one of the best examples by comparison to others they know. So, you could then ask them to name those whom they regard as better than you, and you could widen the assessor population both inside your company and out. Through these two supplementary actions you may be able to establish the names of the individuals whose performance standard could become a target for you, those who are rated at 9.5 and 9.6. Now you will have a goal.

But let's widen this examination even further. Let us suppose that you are the best project manager in your group. Then ask yourself and others:

- Who are among the best project managers in your whole department?
- Who are among the best project managers in your region?
- Who are among the best project managers in your organization worldwide?

And then:

- Who are considered to be among the best project managers outside of your organization?

I suggest that these are the individuals from whom you could learn a great deal. Which professional project manager associations could you join? What professional project management qualifications are available? Could you become a member or fellow of a professional body?

Do you see what I mean? To get a higher score next time, you will need to learn from those even better than you. Who are they? Where are they? How will you make contact?

Now let's drop the word project!

- Who is the best manager in your department?
- Who is the best manager in your region?
- Who is the best manager in your organization worldwide?

And then:

- Who are considered to be among the best managers outside of your organization?

Which professional management associations could you join? What professional management qualifications are available?

To be a better manager means that every month you consciously seek out ways to improve your own management competence.

Every year you attend a business school course for at least a week or two, networking with other talented individuals who want to improve. And every year, you ask your people, peers and boss to complete a 360° feedback report about you and then reflect upon the conclusions.

In short; how much time and money are you investing in you?

Last year I spent   £/$............... on my own development

This year I will spend   £/$............... on my own development

Next year I will spend   £/$............... on my own development

There are probably thousands of potential world champions in every conceivable discipline and field of activity. But the majority of exceptionally talented people fail to put in the time, the hard work and dedication required to become recognized as a role model or world beater. Later in life, independent observers may comment with regret, that he or she "failed to realize the promise they showed earlier in their careers". Focus on your strengths and watch as the weaker parts of your game fall by the wayside as you increasingly become sought out for advice and guidance based on those strengths.

So, ask yourself the question: "What do you regard as your one or two greatest strengths?"

My greatest strengths

1

2

To improve them, please consider your next three steps:

To get even stronger

1

2

3

Regarding your weaknesses? Everyone has them. So, ask others who have as their strengths your weaknesses, to help or alternatively, limit and mitigate their impact on your performance.

> ### *Your* Moment of Power
>
> When you choose to focus on your strengths (and not dwell on your weaknesses) and select your mentor carefully from those who display the same great strengths that you do.

YOUR TIME

6.1   Invest your time – don't spend it!

Or to echo Section 5.2 – manage don't operate. Too simplistic, I know, but if you are to achieve an extra 1% of output, you will need to focus your attention on those items that will bring the greatest rewards. Perhaps you need to think about swapping people between jobs, or changing a process or procedure.

Many managers make the mistake of thinking that they need to be busy, or be seen to be busy; spinning many plates in the air is either their duty or a sign of their importance to the organization. I question that assumption. Sometimes, hyper-activity may mask a lack of confidence.

You know how lawyers and some other professionals charge for their time? Well, start thinking the same way and use the table below to identify the activities that consume the majority of your time every month and allocate a percentage of the time you spend on each. Aim for a total of at least 90% – 95% of all the work you do.

NUMBER	ACTIVITY	% TIME

Looking at this table, now think about how much of your time is spent reacting to something or someone, and how much is proactively spent stimulating the reaction of others around you, including bosses.

REACTIVE % .... *PROACTIVE %* ....

When you examine this division of your time – does it look right? Are you satisfied that this has been the best use of your time? It has, great! If not, what should the division have been to increase the output of your team by 1%?

You can't manage time – it manages you. Don't let the urgent, crowd out the important. Many people have a "start doing list" (complete monthly report, arrange to meet Tony, learn Chinese etc.). That's almost universal, but in order to do those things, you have to forgo others. Do you have a "stop doing list"? Why not put "stop doing . . ." on your "start doing list"?

And finally, how much "thinking time" do you currently invest in your job? And would that be by design or by accident? Continuing with conventional views leaves every manager vulnerable to disruptive industry developments and technologies.

Your Moment of Power

When you stop doing things that are easy for you – either by getting others to do them or by abandoning them altogether – and start investing your time wisely so that you can contribute more to the bigger picture.

6.2 Protect yourself against time stealers

You've decided to start investing your time and not spending it? Great! Now you need to protect yourself against the people and the activities that steal a lot of your time.[1]

For all of the thousands of managers that I have had the pleasure of working with over the years, these are the three top time stealers:

1. People.
2. Email.
3. Meetings.

1. PEOPLE

Some of your people need more of your attention than others. Their personality may require them to get a regular acknowledgement from you that what they are doing is correct. Do they need to be "energized", "encouraged" or "motivated" by you? Whatever the reason, be careful that they don't drain too much of your energy. If they are too demanding it may mean that they are stopping you from becoming a better manager. In that case, will you let them continue?

> "John, I feel that we could improve our working relationship a little for the better. I am conscious that we do interact frequently and although I value the time I spend with you, I would like to understand from your perspective why that is. I am asking you now because I have some major time commitments coming up shortly and I am not sure that I can give you as much time as you normally want. I'm sorry."

Some bosses need more attention from you than you consider appropriate. Some of them are micromanagers, feeling the need to frequently check on you and your work. Will a conversation help? So long as it's cordial and is taken at a time when there are no looming deadlines, it can't hurt.

> *"John, I'd like to raise an issue that has been bothering me for a little while. Because of your frequent requests for updates on progress, I get the feeling that I could do more to make you feel comfortable with what I am doing. What is it about me or my work that makes you feel a little uneasy? What changes do you want me to make to improve our relationship?"*

2. EMAIL

I have not worked for or with a company where email discipline has been strong. I hope that your organization is an exception. Most of the people I speak with bemoan the time that is stolen from them reading through a substantial number of email messages and attachments every day, many of which add nothing to their endeavours or knowledge.

Many people feel the urge to quickly scan an incoming email to see if it is relevant to their work or task at hand. But if they do this their mind is taken off the work they were doing, resulting in a loss of concentration. It's so easy to lose sight of the management job of pursuing the extra 1%.

Ask yourself this question:

Do you read emails according to a time and duration of your choosing, or do emails divert your attention away from potentially more important work? Again, does the urgent, crowd out the important? Answer – have a think about adopting a model for handling/dealing with your inbox. So, what about dealing with your inbox 0800 – 0900 hrs, 1200 – 1230 hrs and 1600 – 1700 hrs? Remember to let people know before you adopt a new system, otherwise they may think you're ignoring them.

As with every rule, there is of course the exception. There will be industries where it is impossible to operate these kind of email time slots. I'm thinking particularly of the financial services sector, where the instantaneous passing of information is an absolute priority for the company's survival. And there will be other circumstances where copying people in via email can establish an essential audit trail.

3. MEETINGS

One of the best ways to waste time, or have it stolen from you, is by attending meetings, both your own and those of others. Meetings tend to use up time in 30-minute slots; one slot or two, and occasionally more. From my experience most meetings don't start on time, don't finish on time and deliver little value to those attending. But your meetings could be different. Instead of having to face working a little later because of the time taken for the meeting, ask yourself if your attendance and extremely valuable contribution is really necessary, and if so, could you send an email or ask a deputy to deliver it?

And finally, when it comes to utilizing your time more efficiently, challenge your own tendency to say "Yes" too often. You can say "No" politely:

"Of course, I'd love to help, and as soon as I finish ... I'll be right with you."

In order to get work completed efficiently and quickly, I have heard of one company that operates a coloured desk-card system to indicate a person's availability:

- Green card visible on the desk – "I'm available to work with you."
- Yellow – "Only approach about Project Z."
- Red – "Do not disturb for a little while, I must finish this."

Yes, it's open to abuse, but a good manager will spot this and deal with the freeriders, so it may be worth a try.

What or who are your 3 greatest time stealers?	Action needed to reduce their impact
1	
2	
3	

Your Moment of Power

When you fit requests from colleagues to use your time into your schedule and not into their schedule.

6.3 Listen more than you talk

Climb into your helicopter regularly. Listen to your staff, especially front-line staff, because they know precisely where the bottlenecks and system failures occur.

This is why I enjoy watching TV programmes where the CEO leaves the boardroom and becomes a trainee on the shop floor. Universally, they appear to learn so much about their own products, their own procedures and in the majority of cases the huge commitment of their people to overcome the shortfalls of the organization, as well as their frustrations that they can't do more.

As well as listening to others, listen to yourself. "You'll never be as good as your sister," played often enough will convince some people that they never will be as good as their sister. Eventually they will say to themselves, "I'm not as good as my sister." For others however, the statement "You'll never be as good as your sister," would act as a stimulus to greater effort, with some so determined to prove their parents or others wrong that it becomes a life goal. Psychologists call this verbal self-guidance. It works in both the positive and the negative. The level of your self-confidence can often determine the level of risk that you are prepared to accept.

Separately, I remember Niall Quinn, the ex-Ireland international footballer and ex-Chairman of Sunderland Football Club, saying to me during a filmed interview that you should try to take every setback as a motivator, mentally reinforcing their power to the point where you say to yourself:

> "I am the one who can do this. In fact, I was born to do this. I will stand tall, accept the knock-backs, but kick on and do what is necessary to achieve the goals I have set."

This is positive verbal self-guidance and requires listening to the one person you often ignore most of all . . . yourself.

> ### *Your* Moment of Power
>
> When you talk yourself into a more positive frame of mind by counting your blessings both at home and at work.

6.4 Infect everyone around you with your upbeat mood and positive attitude

Some years ago, sitting in a railway carriage at Cambridge station, England, I was joined by Bob Satchwell, the executive director of the Society of Editors in the UK. I was on my way to meet some senior executives to discuss leadership issues, and I asked Bob, "Who is the best leader you have ever met in your business?" Answer: "John, you may find this a bit hard to understand, but one of the best that I know is Piers Morgan." "Explain please," I asked. "Well," said Bob, "I read all of the papers every day and you can tell by the way the articles are written – certainly in the Daily Mirror – what sort of mood the editor was in yesterday. Was he upbeat and positive, radiating sunshine; or was he morose, annoyed, irritable? Piers comes out best."

I was amazed – not about Piers, but that the keystrokes of journalists could be affected by the editor walking past. Incredible![2]

You, as the leader and manager, are under the microscope every second of every day. Imagine your mood to be a virus. You infect people with it, and in turn, they infect others. So what does that mean? It means that you must force yourself to be an actor – because your attitude, words and demeanour affect everyone. Appear happy and in control, relaxed even, especially when there are major issues to deal with, and smile (genuinely) more often. People will smile back. Infect them. Every time you enter the building, office, or meeting – set the tone immediately.

> I strongly recommend that you read *Social Intelligence and the Biology of Leadership* by Daniel Goleman and Richard Boyatzis. It's a Harvard Business Review article, Reprint R0809E.

You're sending signals, transmitting permanently – so it's vital to send motivating messages – especially when work is in short supply; just like a virus, innoculate yourself against a downbeat and dispirited boss. Control your own emotions; don't let anyone else control them. Sounds simple, but imagine yourself rudely cut up by another motorist, do you go for the horn, or the finger, or both? Or do you remain relaxed and stay as content and happy as you were before his or her manoeuvre?

So, identify the events that habitually cause you to move into a positive frame of mind, where you feel fantastic and energized to make things happen: hitting a major milestone at work or at home; a "thank you" note from a respected colleague; even a specific piece of music, or the dialogue in a particular film clip. Whatever it is, understand and accept its power on you, and be ready to recall it mentally when you feel a little low. In short, know what lifts you.

So, knowing what lifts you, ask yourself what events or people cause you to move into a dispirited state, where you feel a little cut off and unable to influence things? Identify them, but now try to re-classify them – this time where these same factors are able to motivate you. Sounds simple, eh? But you control your own emotions. Don't allow yourself to be saddened or depressed by other people or events. Instead be disciplined with external stimuli.

A participant on a two-week development programme, offered this example to illustrate the point about control:

> *"John, on the day that I was due to fly here for the programme, I knew that I was going to be tight for time because of work commitments. This meant that I only had a short time for dinner before leaving my home for the airport. So, I phoned my wife and asked her to have dinner ready for when I got home and not to wait until I arrived before preparing it. I finished my meetings and arrived home to find that my wife had not started dinner. SHE*

MADE ME SO ANGRY. Having listened to our discussions, I now realize that I made myself angry. I allowed my wife's actions to control my emotions."

It's so easy, isn't it, to blame other people or events? Too convenient.

A leader leads by example, whether he intends to or not, so it is imperative that your deeds match your words precisely. You cannot say one thing and do another. Your behaviour must reflect your values and principles. You have to be consistent in deed and word.

Your Moment of Power

When you control your emotions to show that you understand the feelings of your people in that moment and can describe a positive way forward.

YOUR IMAGE

7.1 Forget about being liked

Most newly appointed managers, and many experienced ones, demonstrate a tendency through their deeds and words to court popularity. Most people want to be liked.

It can be particularly noticeable when someone from within a team is promoted to become the team's new boss. Up to that moment, that person's relationship with their teammates has been on the basis of equality. Suddenly, the working relationship changes and both sides need to think about, and develop, a new relationship, where the boss perhaps doesn't get to keep the same confidential or even conspiratorial interaction they enjoyed before. The new boss will need to distance himself or herself from the team.

Forget about being liked. You're the boss – even if they don't like you – you're the boss. Focus on the outputs and results – where will you get the extra 1%? For many managers, in many different contexts, it may be more effective to be feared rather than loved, and effectiveness is the only metric.

Can you be effective and loved? Of course you can. But the love will come from the good that you do, the rightness of your actions and your ability to make people happy at work.

And it would be understandable, whilst adjusting to new roles and responsibilities, to copy the behaviour of other managers you have known or the behaviour of managers in your current organization. But the last thing your new people want to see is falseness or a thin veneer of pretence.

Your followers want you to be yourself, to be you. They don't want you to pretend to be something you're not. They want a real person, with all of his or her faults. The last thing they want to see is more of the power-hungry game player, the bully or the sycophant. They've probably had enough of those already!

I've often heard the phrase: "It doesn't matter if they (the team) don't like you, so long as they respect you." It's better if they do, obviously, but I have a suspicion that you can still get an extra 1%, even if they don't respect you, although I do acknowledge that it will be harder.

I heard of one manager who inherited a severely dysfunctional team whose people found it difficult to work together. Previous managers had tried all styles of management to get productivity and output up, and failed. This new manager tried switching between styles and got the same poor results, so he deliberately set out to get each and every member of his team to dislike him intensely. To hate him. For the first time in years, the team united in their hatred of this man and output increased noticeably. Now that's what I call management!

You should not have a fixed management style. Instead, you should employ the management style that is appropriate for the moment. For some people that will mean delivering many more "Well done's" than you believe is warranted, simply to keep the employee productive, while for others you may need to be far more directive than you feel is deserved if you are to get more productivity.

Sitting at the back of one seminar recently, I asked one of the company's directors, sitting next to me, if he personally knew many of the programme's participants. He identified those he did, remarking that one very successful manager needed a good kicking in the mornings to get any work done. The appropriate management style detected and then delivered. Perfect!

Your Moment of Power

When you abandon the attraction of being liked and instead focus on both individual and team output.

7.2 Don't undermine yourself

I have heard many managers subvert their own authority and status within the company by identifying with their team and not the organization they serve. "I've tried to get authorization to proceed, but you know what they're like, they won't buy it." You work for the organization, not the team, so publically align yourself with the company and its policies. If you disagree with them, argue against them privately.

An example. It's annual bonus time, and you have been allocated a pot of money to share among your people. Your boss asks for your judgement on how it should be distributed, and you respond with your draft allocation. But your boss doesn't like one of your team and unilaterally cuts their particular bonus down by 80%. What do you do? Yes, you go back and argue your case, but your boss isn't having any of it, so you call this individual into a private meeting and you have two options as follows:

> Option 1 – "I've tried to get you a bonus of £5000 which I think you deserve, but our lords and masters won't have it. I'm sorry, it's only £1000."

> Option 2 – "I've decided to award you £1000 bonus. I know this will be a big disappointment for you but let me tell you why I have reached my decision. I hope you will take my comments on board and show me more next year so that I can award you £5000."

Option 1 is the easy way out, it's the real situation, but you run the risk of making yourself appear weak and powerless.

Another example would be at the start of a financial year when you have been given stretching new performance targets to say either "I have agreed to these targets" or "They have imposed them".

Us or them? Think about how you communicate the football (soccer) results of your favourite team; "we won", you identify with the win, but "they lost", you disassociate yourself.

I strongly recommend that you think hard about this point, but don't take the point to extremes – if a company decision or management request doesn't align with your values and principles, or worse, diametrically opposes them, you will need to consider seriously your position. Is a change of organization necessary? Your values and principles should never be compromised.

Your Moment of Power

When you make sure that everyone believes that you make all the decisions, not a nameless or faceless higher authority.

7.3   Share your issues and problems

Sitting at your desk and wondering how you can overcome something, or, more positively, seize a new opportunity, is only using one brain: yours.

As an alternative, capture the situation as a briefing paper and then ask others for their ideas and suggestions. Then many brains will be working for you.[1]

You can then evaluate the returns, taking the most attractive elements from each and combine them into your preferred solution. The practice doesn't just work with people at more junior levels. Consider delegating sideways and even upwards in appropriate circumstances.

Delegating responsibility for developing potential solutions and options is how the internet has grown and how many other great ideas have been born from companies as diverse as Google to 3M.

And people like to help nice people. But don't make it one way. You need to "pay it forward" or reciprocate. Most people will respond to:

"I really need your help for a moment" with *"What can I do for you?"*

But, and it's an important but, don't forget to acknowledge the help you received when finally you communicate your decision, otherwise you may not get the same level of cooperation the next time you ask for it. Name everyone who you asked for help, even if they didn't offer any. Why? Because next time, they will!

And consider sending a short handwritten "thank you". If you manage your helper over a distance, then a "thank you" card sent through the snail mail will be far more powerful than a quick email. It shows that you took the time and trouble to do it.

Always use your own handwriting, not typeface, it's far more personal and intimate. I have known very successful managers that use handwritten notes and letters as their key motivator for the extra 1%. It's also the one practice that cannot be delegated.

If you and your team have a connection with an end user or consumer community, then another source of input can be considered: "crowdsourcing". By using social networks carefully, potentially valuable intelligence can be obtained about future designs, colours, services, even prices. However, security is always an issue as you are in the public domain – and your competitors are watching.

Your Moment of Power

When you invite others to contribute to your solution, thank them, and then acknowledge their contributions publicly.

7.4 Express your opinion – otherwise others will assume you don't have one

If you took over from your boss, what would you change and why? Have you got the argument together? Have you got the data to support it? Have you used the 50% of your time "managing" as we saw earlier, and reasoned that an extra 1% could be achieved if the workload was reorganized between you and your peer group? Or the inputs to your team were modified slightly?

If yes, then are you putting forward your ideas? If not, why not? I bet your world isn't perfect.

So, do you believe that your boss has the right priorities? Have circumstances changed enough to warrant an adjustment to the allocation of resources between groups? A five-year plan may run into trouble in year one or even month one. Who will call it? You?

You may consider regularly questioning the strategy and tactics of the wider group in your own mind; the helicopter view again. If the data supports your conclusions, then consider socializing your ideas for the future with others, asking them to comment. It is important to collect opposing and alternative solutions – it will help you to see how others view the same situation and it might help you to form an improved proposition.

As we will see later, many teams perform better if someone in the group regularly asks the hard questions, like "are we heading in the right direction?" And be prepared for "John, I agree that we need a rethink, but now's not the time to rock the boat." There are many age-old excuses for not acting or moving when the data suggests otherwise!

But perhaps you are too politically correct to step out of line; one of the company "yes-men"? I have to confess that on several occasions over the years, I have bitten my tongue and kept my head down. Wife and children to support, a mortgage to pay, it's only human; too risk averse perhaps.

> ### *Your* Moment of Power
>
> When you don't run with the pack but develop your own ideas and socialize them.

YOUR IDEAS

8.1 Expect your ideas to be ridiculed

Using 50% of your time at work "managing" instead of operating will invariably lead you to consider making adjustments to the way the team works or the resources it has at its disposal. You prepare the case for change and present it to your boss.

> *"Listen John, we've tried that before, it was a disaster." "Don't be so ridiculous." "Are you mad, John?"*

Whenever you make unsolicited plans for change, expect an immediate and hostile reaction, similar to the quotes above. Why? Because it will be your boss's way of testing your belief in, and commitment to, your recommendations. So, prior to rolling out your ideas, you may wish to plan your response to these likely critical rejoinders.

Obviously you will fight your corner, and your boss will expect you to. Indeed, you may need to keep fighting it for days or even weeks. Your boss may secretly love your ideas, but he or she knows that the chances of them being successful will depend largely upon your passion, your commitment and the energy you put behind the whole endeavour. By initially rejecting your proposals, your boss is hoping to build that commitment in you to an irresistible level, rather like an archer drawing the bowstring to great tension. Then, when your boss finally gives you the go-ahead, you fly like the arrow, overcoming any opposition or resistance in your path.

And when hearing suggestions from your people, be they half-baked or brilliant, consider initially rejecting them:

"Don't be silly" or *"I don't think so, Kevin."*

Then go back after a day or so and say:

"I've been reflecting on what you said the other day Kevin, and your ideas for making a change. I think you may be on to something here. Maybe there's something in what you say after all. Why don't you give it a little more thought, and especially about the knock-on effects on other departments, then come and see me a in a few days' time. We can discuss it further."

Enjoyment can be significantly increased if initially denied.

Your Moment of Power

When you fight for your ideas and get your people to fight for theirs.

8.2   Start and finish intriguingly

When presenting your ideas or making contributions to team discussions, try to remember what psychologists refer to as the power of "primacy and recency".

This was a tip I was given by Robin Oakley (former European Political Editor at CNN International) about 10 years ago, and I have tried to leverage it ever since when standing up before an audience. The "primacy" element means that, in order to get the full attention of others, you need an opening statement of about 30 seconds that is so powerful, interesting or unusual that it cuts through the audience's immediate thoughts and activities so that they then focus on you and your words to the exclusion of everything else.

The "recency" element suggests that you finish your contribution with another 30 seconds at least as strong as your start, perhaps echoing the main elements of your opening remarks. An example of "primacy" from a participant on a recent development programme:

> "John, I have a very recent example of this – I presented a learned paper to industry colleagues at a university seminar the other day and started my presentation with, 'I bet that I'm the only person here today who arrived on a bicycle.' Later that evening in the bar, I was approached by many people who all said, 'You're that bloke who arrived on a bike aren't you?' They couldn't remember my name or what I spoke about, but they did remember the bike!"

Your Moment of Power

When you grab the attention of others by choosing words and phrases that may initially seem disconnected from their expectations.

8.3　Make your actions speak louder than your words

It's vital to plan ahead, it's great to analyze, and it's important to budget. All very necessary. But "doing things" is more important and, ultimately, the only true test of any well-planned ideas.

And it doesn't matter if what was done turns out to be wrong – unless you're a surgeon it can be changed. I referred to "start doing" lists earlier. Everyone has them, and for many people the same things can remain on their personal lists for quite a while. They never quite get around to doing anything about them. Eventually they're scratched from the list, "it's too late now" or "next year". Do today's stuff today, because tomorrow you'll have tomorrow's stuff to do.

One of my previous managers used an unusual traffic signal message to deliver the same intent. Red, green, amber.

- Red – inactive.
- Green – full-on active.
- Amber – after a while step back and review what is happening and modify your decisions and actions appropriately.

At Facebook, I believe "Run fast. Break things" is commonplace. In the early years at Google, "Near enough is good enough." As with any rule, taken to extremes it can blow back and cause major problems. However, seen and used in its proper place, running with an idea is often the only thing between you and someone else picking it up before you.

I once had the privilege of interviewing the chief executive of a major City of London financial institution, and a phrase he used during our time together has stayed with me ever since:

"John, our mission is to out-execute our competitors every single day."

Figure 8.1

Your Moment of Power

When you set a fast pace and encourage others to join you.

8.4 Collect "yeses"

During all of the development programmes that I and my colleagues have delivered, we have said to the participants that they should feel free to raise any subject they wish for detailed group examination. This means, in some circumstances, that company policies and the behaviour of their senior executives are put under the microscope and questioned critically.

To make the participants comfortable with sensitive issues, we ask everyone to agree that "anything that is discussed within these four walls should remain within these four walls" (the so-called "Chatham House Rule"). General murmurings of agreement and the nodding of heads follows. But that is not enough for us.

To ensure collective responsibility with subjects of critical importance or confidentiality, we go around the table and ask each individual:

> *"Do you agree to keep the opinions expressed during our discussions and the identity of the persons making them private to this group?"*

We then collect the "Yes" from every individual in turn. Why? Because there is a proven link between what people say and their subsequent actions. Robert Cialdini (Regents' Professor Emeritus of Psychology and Marketing at Arizona State University) calls it "consistency". Saying "Yes" out loud in the presence of colleagues cements and strengthens their commitment to deliver what they have promised.

Which means that you have to wait for an unequivocal "Yes" to these types of question:

- "Will you tell me as soon as things look as if they are going wrong?"

- "Will you tell me immediately the results come through?"
- "Will you collect these items on your way to work tomorrow?"
- "Do you think this is the right way forward?"

Even at home, the "Yes" is equally powerful. When your child is going out, don't tell them to "Make sure you're back by 11 o'clock", instead ask them "Will you be back home by 11 o'clock?" and wait to collect their "Yes".

Do not accept silence as agreement or compliance. It isn't!

Your Moment of Power

When you no longer accept silence as an acceptable answer and have the courage to explore the "yeses and noes" of your people.

8.5 Under promise and over deliver

Jean Béliveau, who captained the Montreal Canadiens franchise to six Stanley Cup titles, credited his success on the ice to his off-the-ice mantra: "Know what you're capable of and always under promise so that you can over deliver."

Contrast that tenet with what Willie Walsh of British Airways said when London Heathrow's Terminal 5 opened. I remember him saying that "It will completely change the customer experience forever." It did, but not quite the way that Willie had meant. Unfortunately, for a few weeks after it opened, the customer experience was for the worse with baggage handling and signage coming in for the most immediate criticism. Naturally there was much press comment and some public finger pointing between those involved. Many companies operate within a "blame culture".

Upon reflection, it may have been better to have said: "When we have ironed out all the teething problems on this ground-breaking building, it will completely change the customer experience for the better. But bear with us for the first couple of months (or several months) whilst we work through any unforeseen issues. Hopefully there won't be too many."

And it's a universal phenomenon. In Europe, many cruise ships set sail on their maiden voyage with tens of fitting teams still at work inside the hull, and from the US, we have the Boeing 787. This entered commercial service on 26 October 2011, but was originally planned to debut in May 2008.

I'm sure that when asked for a completion or delivery date, many people genuinely want to help the other party achieve their particular goal, and reply with what can later be considered as an optimistic forecast. But what happens is that the others take your estimate as a given, plan their subsequent actions and give another optimistic date to their customer. It happens with money estimates as well, forecast turnover, profit, etc. Bolt a number of these optimistic estimates together and you have a recipe for disappointment and recrimination. In some cases, even dismissals. If you decide to shoot for a more optimistic date, the risk is that you may need to go back and ask for more time, perhaps more than once, risking damage to your reputation.

But let's consider the alternative. Instead of a response which falls on the more optimistic side of the curve, you offer a longer lead time. Normally, more senior managers become involved at this stage, mandating that a certain date be hit. This is rarely a motivational dialogue because it means you will have to postpone home life activities.

So what's the answer? Well, you may wish to consider offering a range of dates and times, letting the other party decide what numbers to use.

> *"I will be able to get that proposal/estimate to you by close of play next Wednesday or Thursday."*

Of course, delivery at 0900 hrs on the Friday morning is not good enough. Reputation damaged.

Contrast that with offering *"close of play on Friday"* and deliver on the preceding Thursday. Reputation enhanced.

Under promise and over deliver.[1]

Your Moment of Power

When you impress with results and not the promise of results.

Part Three

Your Team Is What You Make It

YOUR INTERACTIONS

9.1 Make your employees happy!

"John, we don't necessarily need happy people, we need productive people. I don't mind if they're miserable, I just need the work
completed." You can hold a stick over people to get the work
done, but I suggest that by focusing on making your staff happy
in their work, it will lead to even more output. The extra 1%
perhaps.

Consider putting employees before customers and before shareholders. Yes, you read that correctly! Put your people first. Make
them feel special. Make them happy. The theory being that if your
people are happy it will make the customers happy and they in
turn will make the shareholders happy. And you won't be alone.
The "employees first" mantra is gaining support in some major
organizations.

Almost all organizations, large or small, have an unbelievable
ability to create processes and practices that restrict people's
natural talents and their authority, thereby limiting their abilities
and enjoyment. Just think for a moment of your current team
and list the restrictions that both you and your organization have
imposed on them: start and finish times, spending limits, personal telephone calls etc.

Then ask yourself the question: "Why?"

I suggest that most of your people have a life outside of their workplace and they seem to manage the huge variety of their responsibilities reasonably well. Make the working environment of your team as rewarding and enjoyable as possible. The effective manager's job is to create the right atmosphere for the staff to excel. With fewer rules, would they really behave any differently? If you actually let them start and finish at times of their choosing and remove all spending limits, do you really think they would only come in just for an hour or two, or buy a new company car with the petty cash?

If you don't trust the people, change the people. If you do trust them, let them go, release their talents and their energies. Then you may be able to sit back and admire your management skills![1]

And don't forget the spouse or partner and home life. How much do you know about the people who work for you? Most people don't perform well at work if they are experiencing problems in their private life, and will contribute more if they are happy with life in general.

The more you know about a person's state of mind, the more you will be able to not only influence their performance at work, but be able to truly empathize. This means making an investment of time. Your time. Time with each of your people. This investment can be as simple as listening to their view on the world, a problem or opportunity at home; in sharing your vision and plans for the future; or in something as simple as attending the funeral of an employee's close relative.

What more can you do to help your people? Or to acknowledge the pressures they may be under?

Investing time in your employees is the surest way to help them towards something that they helped to create – a success.

Your Moment of Power

When you ask yourself what you could do to make each of your staff happier, and then do it.

9.2 Don't wait until they knock on your door

Because you should have already spotted or detected a potential issue or problem and pre-handled it with sensitivity. Quote from Brian McDermott, manager, Leeds United Football Club: "I watch body language, scanning all the time, looking for indications."

The degree of success that people enjoy at work is closely aligned with their level of emotional intelligence. You may have highly developed emotional intelligence, the ability not only to understand yourself and your behaviour, but to sense instinctively the moods of others, or a group of people, and respond to them appropriately.

The more you can instinctively feel the atmosphere around the team, the better. Some of you may find that connection more difficult to make than others, and I would urge those to seek out a professional coach who may be able to help. Or get yourself a copy of *Emotional Intelligence 2.0* by Bradberry and Greaves, the best book I have read on using EI in a business context.

The "manager" in you will watch for body language and try to determine the mood of each *individual* on your team, whereas the "leader" in you will try to determine the mood of the *group* as a whole. If the mood is good, resist the temptation to walk away, satisfied that all is OK; instead try to think of ways that the mood may be enhanced even further.

On the other hand, it is important that you approach any darker moods with sensitivity, treading very carefully to avoid making whatever situation exists even worse. I strongly recommend that you try to bottom out the negative issue or issues affecting the individuals or group as soon as you become aware of them.

If, however, the group is upbeat but one person is "down in the dumps", consider making a discrete enquiry of one of their colleagues:

"John seems very quiet this morning?"

Your Moment of Power

When your emotional radar picks up a signal that one of your people is either dispirited or elated and you respond appropriately.

9.3 Give and show more trust

A true story. Every year, Jane, a partner in a firm of accountants, had the responsibility of auditing her most annoying and ungrateful customer. Every year past, she had tried harder and harder to get a vote of thanks and a verbal compliment on her performance from them, but none had ever been forthcoming. As she sat in the bath one evening, contemplating the next audit which was fast approaching, she had a Eureka moment. Instead of putting her best people on the job, she would put her weakest. They would fall short of the client's expectations, the client would find an alternative auditor, providing excuses for her to dismiss her poorest performers. Then she could upskill her team. A double whammy! She congratulated herself on her wisdom and cunning, topped up her glass of Sauvignon Blanc and relit the aromatherapy candles.

The following day she called her three weakest people into her office and briefed them on the job ahead, warning them that this particular client was the most demanding of all her clients. Four weeks later she arrived at the client's premises to be shown into the boardroom, fully prepared for the worst. The managing director shook her hand, saying "Thank you Jane, best audit we've ever had." Over the next hour, she heard the analysis and recommendations, admitting privately to herself that they were very good indeed.

Back at the office, she called the three in, asking for an explanation. Reluctant at first, eventually one of them asked if he could speak freely, "Of course," said Jane. "Well frankly we were more than a little surprised when you asked the three of us to conduct the audit on your most awkward customer. Sitting together after your briefing, we admitted to ourselves that you could have chosen people with far more experience and reputation. We knew we were not held in the highest regard, and to be honest, we couldn't think why you had trusted us with one of your most important clients. But trust us you did, so we vowed from that moment on to do the very best job that had ever been done and we're delighted to have succeeded. It made us all feel a lot happier at work."

This whole question of trust is terribly important.[2]

Every successful and worthwhile endeavour that I have come across has been based on a high degree of trust. Trust can only be built on a big investment of time and repeated honourable behaviour.

One year, I was working on a project which involved my company cooperating at a senior sales and marketing level with another international company. When getting to know my opposite number, I asked him where in the organization he fitted. He explained that the organization was project based and the project determined who he reported to. Trying to nail it down, I came up with what I thought was a quick and certain way of finding out who his boss was. "So," I asked, "who signs your expenses at the end of every month?" "I do," he replied. "Yes, but who countersigns them?" "No one. I sign them and they get paid." How very, very exceptional and utterly brilliant. Trust. Do your expenses claims have to be countersigned before they are paid?

Not only is there a regrettable lack of trust in many person-to-person work relationships, there is also an obvious distinct lack of trust in many company policies. When illustrating my point on development programmes, I'm often told, "You can't do away with checks and balances, John." I agree, but how this is done is often neglected. Here's a good example of a checks and balance practice from the police service. Public money given to informers has to be accounted for somehow, so the expense claims of police-men and women need to be verified carefully. One newly-appointed district commander was astounded that it took him almost one week out of every four to check all of the expense claims from his people. Operating, not managing. So he changed the instructions, "As from next month, I will go through the three highest claims, line by line, with the claimant sitting with me justifying them. All the rest will get paid without checking." What happened? People tried to avoid being one of the three and the average amount claimed dropped.

What could you do tomorrow to show more trust in your people? Of course, if they have shown that you can't trust them, perhaps you shouldn't be employing them at all!

Your Moment of Power

When you show a lot more trust in people than you naturally think is appropriate.

9.4 Be willing to give people more responsibility than they (or you) expect

If you are in the privileged position of having a number of managers working for you, and one of them leaves or cannot continue in that role for whatever reason, it will be necessary to recruit a replacement. You may be tempted to transfer a person at the same level from another department or recruit externally. Stop. Before you do, read this true story:

"Recently, our Marketing Director was sadly diagnosed with an aggressive cancer and suddenly went into long-term hospitalization. I approached his creative designer and asked if she could take on global responsibility for our group marketing. Her response was 'I'm only the pretty picture girl and have never been asked to participate in a broader role and I have only covered Europe so far, and not Asia and the USA.'

"I explained to her that the responsibilities would include trade and investor websites, exhibitions, brochures/catalogues, PR, customer giveaways, advertising, photography, proactive market research and internal printed staff communication. This was in April 2009. She grasped the opportunity with both hands, and with only two internal junior assistants, has visited Asia, USA and our European sites; consolidated individual country marketing initiatives into a coordinated global strategy; integrated a vast array of message media, some in different languages; introduced Facebook and Twitter and much, much more. All to the satisfaction of our 16 country managers and our main Board. She costs less than half of our long-term absent director (who we continue to support nearly three years after his diagnosis)."

But there is a sequel:

"This new marketing manager went on maternity leave in February 2011 and handed over to her most experienced young assistant. She in turn has performed a rapid transformation under the mentorship of an external marketing consultant on a one-day-a-week

basis. She has entirely carried the weight and responsibility of managing the entire global marketing activities of a £100m+ group operating out of 16 countries – with only a young apprentice assistant!

"She in turn, started her new role on nearly half the remuneration of her temporarily absent manager. Obviously, we have had to rapidly adjust remuneration in both cases, but we are now undertaking a much broader marketing strategy from three years ago for only half the original personnel cost – and the team are highly motivated due to a quantum leap in personal career development, along with progressive and rapid salary rises."

Winners are sometimes disguised by youth and inexperience or simply a lack of confidence! It's your job to get past external predictors of success and see aspects of their potential that they themselves have yet to see.

Your Moment of Power

When you give a lot more responsibility to people than their age and experience would seem to deserve.

YOUR AUTHORITY

10.1 Use your authority wisely

Authority to manage is vested in the role, not in the person who occupies that role. I get irrationally irked when politicians use the words, "my party". It's not their party, it's "the party". The temporary leaders are ships in the night, here today, gone tomorrow.

So it may be helpful if you indulge me for a moment, to consider your authority, i.e. your power to get others to do your bidding, as money in the bank. The question is: Do you draw out the same amount every day, irrespective of your team's performance, or do you vary it according to the team's needs?

Let me offer you two examples at both ends of the authority/ money spectrum:

Example 1 – you have been given a new task and been allocated several people whose skills will be needed to achieve the required goal. For the first few days, perhaps weeks, your new team will need a lot of direction – "do this", "do that" to find their way. Too little use of your authority during this initial period may restrict progress, because team members are new to each other, and they will need to be told what to do in order for them to become productive. At the start of every day, you draw a significant amount of cash from the ATM and spend all of it.

Example 2 – you and your team have been together for a few months in a relatively stable work environment. All of your people know what they have to do each day. They all have their specific roles within the team and they work well together. Using the "do this", "do that" in this scenario, will demotivate them. They don't need to be told what to do. Your people want to make their own decisions. Instead of ordering them about, they need you to facilitate progress, perhaps by making decisions or clearing obstacles from their paths. At the start of every day, you check your wallet before making a withdrawal. You may not need any more money.

So, ask yourself if you are using the right amount of authority for today?

Yes? Brilliant. But when one of your long established team departs and is replaced by a new recruit, you will need to start to draw more cash again. Why? Because many of your existing staff will expect the new team member to fit snugly into the team role of the recent leaver and unfortunately that rarely happens. As a result, there may be overlaps and underlaps of activities as the new joiner finds their best fit within, what is to them, an unknown environment. You will need to consider asking others in the team to adjust their work to accommodate the freshly-arrived talents and skills. During this readjustment phase, it is your job to encourage flexibility within the "new" team, using more of your authority if necessary.

Your Moment of Power

When you resist the opportunity to tell someone what to do and instead let them make their own decisions.

10.2 Sell the need for change before the change

Most of you have experienced change either as an operator or as a manager and, if your experience is anything like the norm, those changes will have taken longer and cost more than originally predicted. So, here are some elements which you should consider for next time.

ESSENTIAL STUFF

You will need time before the change is introduced! For success to take root, the ground needs to be prepared. Unfortunately, many changes are mandated from on high, with very little time between the announcement and the actual change. "Well let's just do it, and do it quickly!" is heard more often than not.

Unless urgency is needed for safety issues, the chances are that people's motivation and their commitment to making change a success will be increased by following all or some of the following rules:

Promote the problem before the solution. Sell it! Make everyone aware of the problem in as many different ways as you can and refer to it regularly. Ask your people for their ideas and suggestions for making the changes. If the plan has been announced, ask for improvements to the plan.

List those people whose work will be affected and what their likely attitude will be. Some will embrace change quickly, others resist strongly. List them in order, with the most resistant last. Why? Because I recommend that you work on them individually, starting with the most amenable to change. Once those are convinced, they will act as your surrogate – selling the new ways to their colleagues in your absence.

Identify the losers. And by that I mean, those individuals who will stop doing stuff. It's likely that they will feel the loss emotionally, because whatever they did, they did with a sense of pride and they thought it was important. They were proud of their work. "In the old days, I used to . . ." So you will need to think about helping them ride through their emotional journey.

Bring the team together frequently and discuss their concerns openly. Staff are usually quick to spot flaws in the proposed solution. "Well what's going to happen to x?" "Who will look after y?" etc. List their concerns and have a response ready for the next get-together. Much of the talk will be about operational issues, but try to get them to talk about their feelings as well.

AVOID

Threats. "John, unless you swing behind these changes and adopt them as your own, maybe this isn't the place for you anymore." Understand that resistance is natural, so instead of making threats, ask for reasons why they have not yet been won over. But do not waver from promoting the change as absolutely necessary, stating your full support for it.

Too much paperwork. Paperwork is impersonal, people can't question the author, may not fully understand the motivation behind the changes or simply misunderstand the written word. Often I have read phrases like this: "In our constant drive to improve customer satisfaction, we have decided to . . ." Phrases like "In our drive to improve customer satisfaction" make the senior managers appear to be disingenuous. It has been used too often in the past as a mask to partially cover unwelcome news. Instead be direct, flood the issue in question with light and analysis, examine different options and then explain the reasons why the chosen course of action was preferred. People may not like the result, but they may come to understand it and grudgingly accept it.

New slogans. Unless the people affected have been directly involved in its development and evolution, avoid catchy phrases. A short slogan has a tendency to put people off and trivialize the issue. "Who on earth thought of that one?"

Once, when I was working for a large multinational company, I became involved in a plan to develop a set of company values. I felt it was necessary to involve as many of the staff as possible; getting representatives to work in a significant number of geographic teams; facilitating cross-team communication and interaction; allowing them to produce a final list of four or five for the board of directors to rubber stamp. I heard nothing for a couple of weeks until I received the five actual values from the board. They had been already decided. Unfortunately (and not unsurprisingly), many of the cynical staff responded with, "Well, let's see how long they live by them." Because the values were handed down from on high, they weren't taken to heart. Avoid slogans.

Badges, coffee mugs, pens and coasters with any new messages. Often these publicity vehicles get widely distributed in the hope that the message on them will be promoted and discussed. It won't, so save your money.

Incentives of any kind. The change should be "the right thing to do". If it is, then the people will gladly accept it. The vast majority of people want to do the right thing.

Keeping existing seating arrangements if the plan calls for new. If people need to be physically relocated then do it as soon as practicable. Retaining existing seating arrangements will slow the change. If at all possible, get the people involved in the new design. The idea being it becomes their design and not yours. But retain a sense of urgency.

So, to summarize, managing effective change is not possible without the appropriate level of preparation and leadership, and leadership isn't meaningful unless it creates significant change.

What do you need to change?

> ### *Your* Moment of Power
>
> When you anticipate and promote the rightness of the change and justify it many different ways, even in the case of a redundancy programme.

10.3 Listen for silence

When making even a very small change, listen for silence.

Why? Because it is likely to be important feedback.

Imagine that you are enjoying a team meeting with your people, discussing the options for a way forward with a particular problem or opportunity, and at some point you propose a solution. "Is everyone OK with that?" Some will undoubtedly say "yes" and others may nod. Others, confident with their analysis, and not afraid to voice their concerns, might say "No boss, I'm not happy with that". Great!

But in some cultures, and with some personalities, you may be met with complete silence from some of your people, or indeed all of them.

Without objections, you may be tempted to think that everyone is comfortable with your proposal. "That's agreed, then." No – stop right there – it's not agreed and they're not comfortable and the only way they can object is by saying nothing.

You should always interpret their silence as a negative response. They disagree with your solution, but, for whatever reason, feel inhibited from giving voice to their objection. Silence is their only weapon.

Don't then ask the flip-side of your first question: "OK – who's not happy with my proposal?" Why? Because some of your team may feel they are being coerced into agreement, even when they're not. For them it's better to "shut up" and get on with it rather than endure a public argument with a more senior colleague.

Instead, if you are faced with this situation, split the group into three or four teams and ask each to record reasons why your solution may not work in the way that you envisage, or risks that appear not to have been acknowledged or mitigated. In a smaller, more intimate team environment, and without your presence, individuals will feel encouraged to state their reservations.

"OK. I have learned that I should always interpret silence as a negative – so, divide yourselves up into four teams and, in turn, tell me two or three reasons why we shouldn't proceed with my proposal. You have 20 minutes."

When you bring the whole group back together, the spokesperson in each team will feel safe and confident with the team behind them, and they will speak up, perhaps revealing drawbacks to your plan that you had not considered.

I would be surprised if you didn't think differently after they have reported back.

Listen for silence.

Your Moment of Power

When you listen for and acknowledge silence as important feedback on your proposal.

10.4 Deal swiftly with conflict and personality clashes

Vigorous debate between team members should be encouraged. The process for getting to a viable and well thought-through plan of action may involve a passionate exchange of opinions and fierce argument. A "dynamic tension" should exist between the people and they should feel free to express themselves vehemently within a "safe" team environment, where recrimination is absent.

Every team needs someone who is brave enough to say, "Why are we even doing this at all?" Now, some managers may categorize these people as a bit awkward, difficult even, but come to value those with a sharper focus on the bigger picture. However, take this principle too far with too many individuals and you may restrict team output, as the people will spend too much time arguing. It's your job to make sure the balance is appropriate.

With your facilitation and occasional direction, the team should eventually come to an agreement and then be united when preparing the execution phases. There should be no residual ill feeling or hostilities once a decision has been reached.

If an overhang of conflict does remain, or if in different circumstances there is a "personality clash" between two of your team members, the situation can rapidly become untenable and may risk undermining wider team morale. Cliques and factions may start to form. People will take sides and you will need to act.

Obviously, you will speak with the people involved privately and confidentially and tell them that, for a harmonious team, they will need to sort out their differences. At first this should be a gentle encouragement, but if the situation persists, then a stark warning may need to be issued:

"I will not tolerate this situation persisting any longer, either you two sort out your differences or your future on the team will need to be seriously considered."

Let us suppose that they make efforts and things calm down for a while but then they flare up again (which is usually what happens). What do you do? At that point, I ask you to consider a challenging course of action. You fire them both, however good they are. I believe the alternative of firing only one risks creating both winning and losing factions within your team, and that could be a recipe for continued low-level disharmony and a more permanent lack of team spirit. The output of the team, may suffer. But by firing them both you make it clear to the rest of your team that you will deal firmly with anything which threatens or weakens the focus on team output and production.

Those who are familiar with the personalities involved in the Enron collapse may have already drawn a parallel.

Your Moment of Power

When you end destructive conflict in your team and demonstrate a measured ruthlessness in dealing with it.

YOUR SUCCESSES
AND FAILURES

11.1 Build confidence by reacting to team wins and team losses appropriately

Every team has its successes and the occasional failure. How do you react to a team success and how do you react to a team failure?

Imagine that you manage a football (soccer) team. Consider and contrast your imaginary post-match debrief with the players after winning 5-0 and after losing 0-5.

I suggest that after losing 0-5, you say little and take them down to the local bar or restaurant, to wash their memories of the disappointment with alcohol. "Forget it" is your message – say nothing to weaken their confidence even further, it will have taken a knock. Don't keep playing the tape over and over on a sequence of poor play. Don't unintentionally reinforce failure and fear in their minds.

But I suggest that after winning 5-0, you keep the players together for hours, running and re-running the same tape, highlighting those recorded ball-passing sequences that led to an exciting victory. Reinforcing success and building confidence.

Forget the bar or restaurant – let them constantly replay their part in the team's success during their drive home.

But of course, you may not run a football team. So at work, debrief and reprise successful outcomes. At an appropriate moment, stop work to celebrate a success. If appropriate, mention each of the team members and explain their contribution to the team's success. Show, and tell them how pleased you are with their collective efforts. Display photos, customer quotes, thank you letters etc. But don't stop with just one celebration. Reinforce success and build confidence yet further by regular reminders.

World championships and Olympic games are festooned with PBs or personal bests. The next time you witness a medal ceremony on television, pay close attention to the expressions of the rostrum trio. Gold medal, happy. Silver medal, disappointed. Bronze medal, surprised and thrilled because he or she didn't expect it.

Working thoughtfully to get the extra 1% of output means that your team will regularly deliver a "personal best". Let them see your delight!

Your Moment of Power

When you reinforce previous individual and team success at every opportunity.

11.2   Celebrate advances fairly

When your team manages to secure their next PB or increase in output, consider how you might acknowledge their success and reward them. You don't have to spend money necessarily, but your team needs to understand that their efforts have been noticed. Often a simple "thank you" is all that is required.

So, what will you do? May I suggest that, whatever it is, you do it quickly, and if the reward is money, back it up with a handwritten note or telephone call. Chances are your little add-ons will be just as motivating as the money. Intrinsic rewards are proven to be much more powerful than extrinsic ones for most people. So use recognition, status, or time off to do something worthwhile as rewards where you can, rather than money or vouchers.

I know of one huge international company where the sales people have to spend an inordinate amount of time calculating and submitting their monthly commission claims. This is challenged and then (like the worst insurers) further justification is sought by higher-ups before a settlement is reached some months downstream. Everyone complains about it, and rightly so. It is a hugely demotivating incentive scheme. A brilliant oxymoron! I suspect an extra 1% of output is within reach but "company policy is company policy, John."

At the end of the financial year, the bonuses of many companies are often decided upon arbitrarily by senior managers, sometimes depending on their regard for the individual. Fairness can be questionable.

At one UK retailer, John Lewis, the bonus pot is divided up so that every staff member is rewarded with an annual bonus of an extra number of weeks' pay. So, for example, everyone gets an extra five-weeks' pay. Once the bonus pool is fixed, fairness is built in. Brilliant!

I also recall a worthwhile scheme, run by a UK trade supplier with a nationwide branch network who set a branch profitability target every month. Any excess was retained within the branch and divided between the staff in a strict and fixed format: delivery drivers came first, then sales assistants, then warehouse staff etc. until, if anything was left over, the branch manager got it. So, if the profit in one month only just exceeded the target, then perhaps only the delivery drivers would get their fixed percentage bonus; if the target was smashed then perhaps the branch manager received enough to buy a small car. The system worked very effectively, and when I turned up at a meeting with all of the branch managers in attendance, the car park was full of high-spec black Mercedes.

Maybe you can re-examine your bonus formula and improve it? Would this help achieve the extra 1%?

Your Moment of Power

When you are seen and heard to be fair.

11.3   Stop rumours by sharing the brutal truth early

If the circumstances of your organization are seriously difficult, and people are fearful for their future – be straight with them. Tell them the truth as you understand it. It may be unpalatable, but honesty is always appreciated. Otherwise, rumour and gossip will abound, causing unnecessary anxiety and stress. Don't be tempted to honey-coat the picture you give them. Instead, be uncompromisingly clear about the problems you all face. People are better at dealing with known risks than they are at dealing with conjecture and uncertainty.

Your people won't know what to do for the best. They will be extremely worried about their job security and the knock-on effects on their home life. In times like these your people will look to you for guidance. "What should we do, John?"

You will need to be seen to be preparing for many eventualities. If the worst happens, and the team is disbanded, are there other opportunities with the same organization? Could some people be transferred to other departments? If not, then potentially which outside companies or bodies may be interested in the skills of your people? If Plan A states that things gradually improve and you all stay together, what is your Plan B and Plan C?

Try to stay upbeat and positive. Paint a picture in the minds of your staff of a better future. But don't go overboard – it has to be believable. And through bad times and good – have a motivating goal that the whole team should be trying to achieve in the next month or two. Twelve-month goals may seem too distant for many people, especially when their job is at stake. Communicate this vision of yours in terms of how they will feel when the goal is achieved. Minimize the "management speak" if you can.

I remember speaking with a factory boss in Birmingham, and I asked him what the production-line workers wanted to know about the business. "Are they interested in the P & L?" I said. "No John," he replied, "all they want to know is the level of the order book and will they have a job tomorrow." Keep your communications grounded.

Your Moment of Power

When you tell your people what they want and need to know as early as possible to stop unfounded rumour.

11.4 Don't shoot the messenger

It is extremely important for you to create an atmosphere where your people are quick to share bad news, or tell you things they think you don't want to hear. Which means that they have to trust that you won't shoot the messenger.

There are few right answers in business, or for that matter in any non-commercial organization, and good bosses want to know the facts, the real conditions, so that they can be encompassed within their thinking. When asked "How's Project X going?" it is not unusual for subordinates to feel constrained with their answer, accentuating the positive and subordinating or even eliminating the negative. You should make it clear to everyone that if one of your people makes a serious mistake, which may have widespread negative repercussions, he or she should have no hesitation in bringing it straight to you.

Similarly, if you make a serious mistake, noticed by one of your staff, you should make it equally clear that they should feel comfortable raising it with you. But, the chances are that, at first, they will socialize their misgivings about your mistake with their colleagues, asking the question, "What do you think we (not I) should do?"

Autopsies on the demise of companies often reference the attitude of a top boss who displayed a tendency to cover their ears when told unpalatable news. But working relationships between bosses and staff can be markedly different in the Far East, where age and seniority make it much more difficult for a junior to question the actions of a senior. Planes have crashed, killing all occupants, in this century because the Asian co-pilot felt unable to call attention to a serious mistake by his or her Asian captain.

Although the importance of *mianzi* (saving face) in the Far East and especially China is well known, the concept can be applied equally and effectively in other cultures. Please consider this aspect during team meeting discussions, as some individuals can feel slighted or disrespected very easily by others and then they may withdraw from any interactions. During your career you may have felt "stung" by an off-hand comment from someone else, who may not have noticed the effect upon you.

So, how do you react to bad news? Do your people feel comfortable bringing it to you?

If brought particularly bad news, you should not allow others or events to infect your positive mood or disposition too often. But it is OK, and recommended by some, when people conspicuously fail to maintain your high standards of conduct, to display the odd flash of anger. It can increase the concentration of your team on their job, and therefore their performance and output. But you should never be angry with anyone in public. When presented with conspicuous failures of others to adhere to your principles and your values, the team should be made aware of your controlled anger, calmly.

Your Moment of Power

When your people show that their trust in you has reached a level high enough for them to bring you bad or unwelcome news quickly.

YOUR MEETINGS

12.1 Don't buy in team building events – do them yourself

I really believe, and have always practised, the management principle that if you have smart people (or at least potentially smart people), it is absolutely essential to create the right environment for them to be able to excel. In an attempt to build the right environment you may consider buying in a team building event or exercise. Please think again.

I've been on many indoor and outdoor team building exercises and greatly enjoyed the vast majority. Most of my colleagues found them to be equally enjoyable. We had a lot of fun, constructing catapults, building river rafts and attempting military style assault courses outside.

Inside, we sang opera, learned to dance and attacked business games.

There was plenty of laughter, fantastic food and the odd glass of vino. Did they help bond the team and contribute towards an extra 1%? Sadly not. Any benefit may have lasted only a day or two at most.

For me they were a waste of time and money, and yet I still occasionally witness a blindfolded person bumping into trees, surrounded by his or her teammates in hysterical laughter.

Save your money.

If you are bringing people who are largely unknown to each other together for a new purpose, getting them to understand one another is important. Whether the new role is a permanent one or a specific project, you may wish to consider splitting them into sub-groups and allocating a non-work subject for them to debate and discuss, e.g. "If we all decided to donate a half-day's pay to a good cause, what would you like to support?" This type of challenge gets people talking about their interests, passions even.

Or if you had a very modest amount of money at your disposal, you could take a look at discovering and discussing their individual preferred *Belbin team-role types*, which is explained a little later. This is followed by two more profiling exercises which you may also find useful to explore with your team.

Your Moment of Power

When you tackle your responsibilities head-on and resist the desire to sub-contract them to external organizations.

12.2   Encourage your people to put on the Six Thinking Hats

Edward de Bono's "Six Thinking Hats" model for determining the best course of action can prove very effective at team level. It's quick and it's fun! So I suggest you read his book and make yourself very familiar with it.[1]

In summary, his "hat" model requires that everyone thinks about a problem, opportunity or project from a number of pre-conceived frames – each hat signifying a different framework for thinking. While each hat is in use everyone is thinking from the same frame as signified by the hat. Why? Because most people have a propensity to think the same, or a similar way, about each and every challenge. Are you a "glass half-full person", or a "glass half-empty person"? De Bono offers an alternative which encourages people to think differently and thoroughly. The Six Hats framework does not encourage people to think differently per se, but rather encourages people to think more constructively, more collaboratively, more intensely, while using the particular focus of each hat.

As a result, people tend to draw better conclusions; look at a problem or issue more holistically and with increased awareness and identify where information is lacking or where further information is required.

De Bono gives each of the six perspectives a colour: red, white, yellow, black, green and blue. Here is an example of a short demonstration of his work that I have used at workshops in the past, having fully explained de Bono's model. With me wearing the blue hat, which sets the focus for the investigation or discussion, I say: "In the next 45 minutes you are all going to redesign your company's logo symbol and strapline. Let's start by putting on our black hats (a kind of devil's advocate approach), and working in pairs, identify and record as many criticisms of your current logo as possible. You have 10 minutes." After that, we work through all the coloured hats in turn until we reach the blue hat again, which requires everyone to bring together all of their work and propose an attractive, workable and well-supported solution.

I had the pleasure of observing Edward de Bono at the London School of Economics in 2009. He started his session with this question to the audience: "Please add the numbers 1 to 10 together. What's the total?" Within a few seconds there were shouts of 55. "Well done," he said, "now add the numbers 1 to 200 together." Laughter for several seconds until someone shouted 20,100. "Correct," he said. Then he explained why he had asked the questions. "With the first question, you probably all started with 1 and then added 2 to make 3 and then added 4 to make 7 etc. until you reached 55, but that is only one way to get the right answer. You could have multiplied 10 by 11 and divided the answer by two to get to 55 via a different thought process. So 200 multiplied by 201 and divided by 2 is still possible mentally to get to the answer of 20,100."

He was showing the audience that there is usually another way to tackle a problem if you go and look for it. Different ways of thinking, as opposed to different thoughts. So, can you identify the best way forward to address your current issues by using his "Six Thinking Hats" methodology? Almost certainly – and it's fun.

Your Moment of Power

When you can think about a problem or opportunity like a scientist (from different perspectives) and make choices based on the outcomes and not on your own bias.

12.3 Use brainstorming and Mind Mapping to generate lots of ideas and options

Two extremely useful methods for developing possible options for a way forward are brainstorming and Mind Mapping.

I have observed many of these valuable exercises where the rules of the game aren't followed. For example, when brainstorming, the idea is to generate as many suggestions as possible. The objective is volume, however crazy some ideas may appear when first heard. Judgement has to be suspended for the first phase of the exercise, otherwise too much time is spent dissecting each suggestion. If suggestions are criticized, some people will feel too inhibited to offer more thoughts and ideas, fearing a slap down. Support all of the offerings with a "thank you". Here are the widely accepted rules of brainstorming:

- Suspend your judgement of ideas.
- Encourage exaggerated and radical ideas.
- Go for volume of ideas, the quality doesn't matter initially.
- Build on the ideas of others.
- Every person and every idea is equally valuable.

An alternative to ideas and suggestions being shouted out and recorded, is to ask that the same ideas and suggestions be written onto Post-it notes by the author and stuck on a board or flip chart. That way, individuals may be less influenced by the direction of the verbal contributions of others. At some point you will need to stop and ask everyone involved to read all of the ideas so that they have the opportunity to add more based on the contribution of their peers.

When the suggestions start to dry up, encourage the participants to combine or re-work some of the earlier ideas into new ones.

Brainstorming can be particularly powerful when thinking of and recording potential risks to a desired outcome and unforeseen effects on unrelated activities.

Mind Mapping is best used as an adjunct or follow-on to brainstorming when, having collected tens or even hundreds of ideas, they need to be organized into groups. The attractiveness of each group can then be examined and compared with the other groups. The following chart (Figure 12.1) could have been drawn in response to the question, "What shall we all do later after our team meeting?"

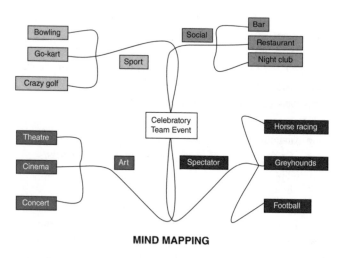

MIND MAPPING

Figure 12.1

Your Moment of Power

When your people see you shining a light onto the path ahead.

12.4 Deal with disruptive behaviour

Meetings are one of the best time and energy stealers available.

Unless leveraging the power of the "Six Thinking Hats" model or brainstorming or Mind Mapping or using a similar model, I recommend that you abandon them, especially those that are held at regular intervals, i.e. monthly. If you need one, a short telephone conference call may suffice. However, let us assume that you are chairing one and observe the following behaviours. You may wish to consider dealing with them as follows:

Interruptions. People should be allowed to finish the point they are making. So:

> *"Let John finish please, then I'll come to you."*

Otherwise John may feel that his contributions are not being taken seriously and may withdraw mentally from the discussion. Then John's commitment to any conclusion may be minimal or non-existent.

Supporters. You may hear supportive remarks such as "great idea, boss" from those who may be trying to ingratiate themselves with you. Thank them for their support but challenge them to think of some of the risks involved, or develop some alternatives.

Taking Over. Occasionally one of your people may decide to flex their corporate muscles and say to the rest of the team something like "I think what the boss is saying is this" and slightly adjust the meaning behind the statement you have already made, taking it onto their agenda. Gently and immediately correct them with:

> *"Not quite, John, but close. Let me say it again."*

Mobile Phone/Texting. The announcement "mobile phones off please for the next 30 minutes" at the start may get some to comply, but others may not and regularly one person will say, "Sorry boss, I'm waiting for an important call." That may or may not be true – so how do you respond? I recommend that whatever rule you decide upon, it should apply to all:

"If you're in the meeting, phones off please. If you can't comply, then please wait outside until you receive the call. Thank you."

Some managers I know have a tariff of fines for non-collegiate behaviour, which to me seems a little demeaning and may make the person being fined feel belittled and resentful.

Silence. We have already discussed how you should perceive silence as a team reaction to your proposals, but there is usually someone who, for whatever reason, appears less involved. With them, I recommend that you say something like:

"Some excellent points, Ladies & Gentlemen. John what do you think of the points made/discussion so far?"

Downbeat. Fortunately, there is always someone in the room who is far more pessimistic than the others about the effect of the initiative under discussion. I use the word "fortunately" because, although their lack of enthusiasm may be a little frustrating at times, they may be right. "I don't think the economy will grow by 3% this year." So:

"You may be right, John, but how would you suggest we mitigate the risks which you think are more powerful than some of your colleagues?"

Some may say, "I don't like that idea." You may respond with:

"I respect your opinion, John, but let us hear how you came to that conclusion. What is your analysis, your reasoning?"

Although "gut calls" should be heard, encouraged even, analysis is usually more powerful than opinion.

Early Doors. Some people will press for an early agreement, "Let's make a decision and go" because to them, there may appear to be more urgent problems. But don't let the urgent things crowd out the important things. Many decisions can't be reached in one meeting; you may need several if there is a lot at stake.

Late Arrivals. Meeting etiquette at many companies is poor, they don't start on time and they run over the time allocation. One manager I know locks the door at the publicized start time, so if people are late they don't participate. Others start and finish at quirky times, start 0957 hrs, close at 1023 hrs. But many managers tell me that their boss, the chair person, is never on time, which is a great way to set a poor example!

Stand Up! Although I have never used it myself, I do know that some managers hold meetings where everyone remains standing. I'm told that it makes for a sharper focus on the subjects under discussion.

And finally – try if possible to finish early.

Your Moment of Power

When you are quietly in control of both the pace and progress of the meeting agenda.

YOUR PEOPLE

13.1 Talk about the different generations

If you have a mix of ages in your team, you will understand already that, in some circumstances, the attitudes and behaviours of the younger people may differ from those older team members. Academics have created three very general demographic categories to help managers better understand the differences between the generations and coined the terms, "Baby Boomers", "Generation X" and "Generation Y". You may already be familiar with the main descriptions of each, but if not, here they are:

Baby Boomer is used to describe a person born after the Second World War and up to about 1960. The baby boomers were the first group to be raised with televisions in the home. The boomers found that their music, most notably rock and roll, was an expression of their generational identity. Boomers often are associated with the civil rights movement, the feminist cause in the 1970s, gay rights, anti-war protests, sexual freedom, and experimentation with various intoxicating recreational substances. Boomers at work are usually industrious, committed and loyal. They possess a strong work ethic and a sense of duty as the breadwinner. Generally, they put themselves last for consideration after their parents and their immediate family. They are prepared to work long hours and have grown up following fairly fixed routines. For many, clocking in and clocking out was a habit for decades.

Generation X is a term used to describe those born from the early 1960s to about 1980. Generation X is mainly noted as one of the most entrepreneurial and technology-savvy generations, as they have driven a majority of the internet's growth. Google, Yahoo!, Dell, YouTube, Apple Inc., and many other billion-dollar technology companies were founded by Generation Xers. They are sometimes called the "sandwich generation", as they may have elderly parents and young children. At work, some Generation Xers tend to be less loyal than the Boomers as they may have become disaffected with politics and ruthless corporate behaviour. The trust they initially placed in people in high positions has gradually evaporated over the years and their cynicism has grown. They take a great deal of interest in the state of our planet.

Generation Y is generally used to describe those born between the early 1980s and the late 1990s. Generation Y or the "iPod Generation", grew up in a time of even less certainty than Generation X, e.g. the 9/11 attack on the twin towers, the credit crisis, failing economies and high unemployment. Social networking has made this generation completely open. They are sometimes portrayed as demanding, selfish, text-addicted job-hoppers with little loyalty to their employers. It is in their nature to challenge authority and the age-old way of doing things. They dislike rigid rules, such as starting and finishing work at set times. But two factors separate Generation Yers from the other generations: firstly, they are usually up to date with the pace of technological change, wanting to use their personal technology devices at work and for work; and secondly, they are experiencing a lack of job security. The Generation Yers are hungry to learn, and are open to mentoring by Baby Boomers, and, helpfully, they can be quick to tell their manager that there is a better way.

The individuals on your team may or may not display the same broadly-painted features as others of their generation or they may be more extreme. But you will find it worthwhile to ask your team to discuss the issue, possibly having flipchart headings such "Things I like about 'Baby Boomers'" and "Things I don't understand about 'Baby Boomers'" and do the same for the other generations. The exercise will help everyone gain a better understanding of their colleagues' personal perceptions/prejudices, which in turn will lead to improved team working.

Your Moment of Power

When you celebrate and leverage generational differences to improve performance.

13.2 Understand the Specialists and Plants of the Belbin model

You can forget the raft-building and blindfolds of ineffective team bonding, and instead, get your team to complete the *Belbin Team Roles Self-Perception Inventory*.[1] This will help them to identify their natural and preferred contribution to the team effort and where they may tend to rely on the contribution of others.

Through this exercise, people can understand better the differences between themselves and other team members. They will identify where they make their biggest contribution and where they depend upon the skills of others.

Meredith Belbin describes what he terms as an "allowable weakness". This can be considered as the price to pay for getting the contribution of each individual, and it is particularly relevant within a team environment as everyone will have an "allowable weakness", including you! Here is an example:

Belbin Team-role Type	Contribution	Allowable Weakness
Completer/Finisher.	Painstaking. Delivers on time. Conscientious.	Inclined to worry unduly. Reluctant to delegate.

The full list of Belbin team-role types is as follows:

- Implementer.
- Completer/Finisher.
- Shaper.
- Co-ordinator.
- Resource Investigator.

- Team Worker.
- Plant.
- Monitor/Evaluator.
- Specialist.

One team-role type is not better or worse than any other. There is no hierarchy. Rather, Belbin says that a team is most efficient when all of the roles are covered naturally. But if there is a gap in one or two types, the work will still get done as the team members will automatically compensate for the missing role or roles.

If you, or an external consultant, outline the work of Meredith Belbin during one of your regular team meetings, it can be very revealing when the individuals share their predominant team-role type with their colleagues. The process can also help you, the manager, because the exercise may identify a gap in the ideal combination of team-role types or indeed a heavy duplication of preferred roles. This may help you when you next need to recruit new people. Maybe the extra 1% could lie here?

Your Moment of Power

When you recognize the predominant team-role type of the people you nominate for a specific task.

13.3 Don't assume that you get the full picture from those far away

Managing people over large distances and time zones is obviously more challenging than if they sit close by. I am often asked by participants on our development programmes if the same management techniques hold good in these circumstances. Whilst a significant majority are valid, there are some key differences.

If members of your team are working alone in the field, and perhaps attached to another department of the same organization for local administrative support, you may wish to consider more frequent contact using Skype®, Windows Live® or similar, so that they continue to feel part of the team and not cut-off from the usual office politics. You may need to feed them with more of the office gossip as well. "John's daughter is pregnant," "Emily's on a new diet," "Phil went to see Arsenal win on Saturday." But asking them "Are you OK?" or "Is everything OK?" may not persuade them to tell you their true feelings. Instead, ask questions which may be more effective at teasing out their true feelings and their issues:

> *"I guess you must have had enough of the place by now?"* or *"How much longer do you want to stay there?"* or *"I don't suppose the locals are giving you enough support?"* or *"What's the biggest disadvantage or frustration you have there?"*

If you have a team working at distance, there is a great danger that the manager of the distant section will protect their "empire" and feed you mainly good news. The way for them to keep you off their backs is to be positive and upbeat: "Everything's great here. Of course, we have our normal share of frustrations, but we're getting to grips with them." Then they may try to throw you off course by asking, "How's John doing over in Alaska?" It is more difficult for the distant manager to admit to making mistakes or to give you an accurate feel for the mood of their team. They may feel that to volunteer the information that morale is low and that too many mistakes are occurring would threaten their own position.

To counter this natural human defence, place one of your trusted people into that team so that you can get as close to the real picture as possible. If that's not possible for whatever reason, then voice your reservations:

> *"John, it would only be natural for you to paint a picture for me of a team well managed, with the people working well together and producing excellent output. I'm a long way away, and I wouldn't know any different, but I need to know the real picture John, with all of the negatives included. I know you'll be addressing them, so, please don't be defensive. You're a good man/ woman – and I know we can work well together. Are you OK with that?"*

Wait for the "yes" and then ask for the top three issues that he has:

> *"Excellent. So what are your top three problems or issues, John?"*

Maintain frequent communication with the manager, as if he or she were working alone in the field as above. But if your under-manager has his own team, provide regular and frequent updates to them on the bigger picture. If a video link is not available, then a personal visit, perhaps every month, may be needed; or a short video chat to camera that can then be emailed to them.

In other jurisdictions, locally employed staff and ex-pats may be on different employment terms and conditions and rates of pay. This situation has the potential to cause problems, so keep a close watch on the local wage averages and consider maintaining a small premium to keep the locals comfortable.

Your Moment of Power

When you encourage distance workers to talk negatively about their circumstances and shine a light onto their concerns.

13.4 Don't tolerate a warm body

When some critical skills are in short supply, I know that many managers keep someone on the payroll even though they may only be operating at 50% of required output because "John, it's better to have a warm body than no body at all."

I couldn't disagree more.

Why? Because of the effects this decision has upon the remainder of the team. They see, perhaps even more vividly than you do, that the person in question is a marginal contributor; not quite good enough. Some may go as far as to question why you keep him or her on the team at all. "Why doesn't the boss do something?"

But the main danger is that if they see you accepting suboptimal performance and low output from one individual, the motivation of the rest of the team may suffer. "I don't see why I should bust a gut, when the boss keeps John on the team! He contributes so little." You could undermine your own authority when you're pushing for the extra 1%.

Compare and contrast the management of your team with a perennially successful sports team such as Manchester United or the New York Yankees. The manager, or coach, is relentlessly searching for the extra 1%. They bring in fresh talent regularly; employ scouts who search for even more effective players; they are always thinking of the composition of the team, never satisfied. Fear of losing can be a great motivator. Even within a single game, you see the coach talking to the players, changing tactics to blunt the opponent's strategy.

But be careful, creating too much turbulence risks damaging team spirit, while too little upheaval means the team stagnates. Do you have the right balance?

Warm bodies – no. Only hot!

Your Moment of Power

When you are ruthless with sub-optimal performances.

Part Four

Your Talented Staff

THEIR PERSONALITIES

14.1 It's your duty to kick and pat!¹

Some people need a good kick up the backside to draw out their best and to get them to work productively, others need a simple pat on the back. If you kick the person who needs a pat, or likewise if you pat the one who needs a good kick, then you decrease their commitment and motivation and in the process reduce your output.

You know which are which already, thank goodness.

People are your biggest resource, your biggest cost and your biggest profit improvement opportunity.

And yes, it is quite possible to kick and pat the same person during the same working day. Be alert to individual needs. Interact with your team members regularly, checking their mood, and thinking to yourself – how can I get that extra 1% out of them?

But your ability to change people significantly is limited. I'm grateful to Marcus Buckingham and Curt Coffman who used this phrase in their book *First Break All The Rules*.²

> "People don't change that much. Don't waste time trying to put in what was left out. Try to draw out what was left in. That is hard enough."

Some managers, even vastly experienced ones, find it difficult to either kick or pat or both. And it would be natural for a newly appointed manager to feel a little uncomfortable, or nervous even, when the need to praise or reprimand one of their team members occurs, especially if that person is older. I use the word "need" because some of your team will have a very real need to be praised or reprimanded in order for them to reach their full potential.

So it's not an option to praise or reprimand for any manager; it's a necessity. It's a duty. So, for those who do find it difficult here's a reminder; keep your comments focused on the performance of the individual and not the person. You can simultaneously praise the person whilst criticizing their performance:

> "You're a really top guy, John, but your performance on Project X (or today) has been below my expectations. I want to find out why you have let yourself down and how we can get back to business as usual."

Look them in the eye; finish with a handshake and tell them how much you appreciate their usual contribution, even if, on this particular occasion, it wasn't up to scratch.

Your Moment of Power

When you "kick" and "pat" at precisely the right moment for maximum effect on output.

14.2 Spread understanding of different attitudes and behaviours through MBTI

You may or may not know your personal four-letter MBTI personality descriptor.[3] For those who don't, you may wish to consider completing a simple, low-cost, online questionnaire which reveals your own personality type, expressed as a code with four letters. Answering the questions reveals your preference in each of the following four categories:

- **Favourite world:** Do you prefer to focus on the outer world or on your own inner world? This is called Extraversion (E) or Introversion (I).
- **Information:** Do you prefer to focus on the basic information you take in or do you prefer to interpret and add meaning? This is called Sensing (S) or Intuition (N).
- **Decisions:** When making decisions, do you prefer to first look at logic and consistency or first look at the people and special circumstances? This is called Thinking (T) or Feeling (F).
- **Structure**: In dealing with the outside world, do you prefer to get things decided or do you prefer to stay open to new information and options? This is called Judging (J) or Perceiving (P).

Your report will show by how much you prefer one dimension to another. For instance, you may be extremely I or extremely E, or sit almost in the middle between the two. There are no right or wrong answers.

I recommend that you consider asking the individuals on your team to complete MBTI, and then to share their profile with their colleagues, perhaps during a team meeting. The benefit is not generally to the individual, the vast majority accepting the validity of their profile, but rather to the team as a whole. By uncovering the MBTI of their colleagues, it will help the individuals on the team gain a better understanding of the actions and stances of their colleagues.

As with other profiling tools, it would help you and your people to have a qualified practitioner on hand for any discussion.

Your Moment of Power

When you explain to your team members the personality differences between them, so that they are better able to work together.

14.3   Put yourself forward for a 360°

A 360° feedback report is an evaluation of one person by his boss, his peer group and his subordinates.[4] That person can then compare their own view of their strengths and weaknesses with the input from the other groups. You should regularly undertake a proprietary 360° to confirm that your own self-image aligns with the image that others have of you. They can be completed online, are relatively inexpensive and provide you with valuable feedback about your own leadership and management skills.

When moving to a new role, consider completing another 360° after a year or so, and roughly every year or two thereafter. A four-year-old 360° report completed with a different team will be of little value to you.

A very valuable development of the usual 360° feedback is the Leadership Dimensions Questionnaire (LDQ) which is a specialized adaption of the typical 360° feedback. It is now recognized as an internationally proven exercise in determining whether the leader's style matches the business context in which the manager is working.

The premise is that a company conducting business as usual will need a different style of team leadership as compared to a company experiencing transformational change. The online questionnaire submissions are processed and a report produced which highlights any differences in perception, and compares the subject's scores with the average of thousands of previous participants, mainly from the western world. But the critical element of the report either confirms that the exhibited leadership style matches the business challenges or points to a possible mis-match between the two.

And if you would prefer to undertake a 360° based upon the principles embodied within this book, go to: www.moments-of-power.com.

And with all of the 360° formats, I would urge that you arrange for a private and confidential discussion with an expert counsellor in person or via the telephone, once you have read and digested the report.

As we saw in the second section of the book, your first responsibility, as a leader and manager, is to understand yourself.

Your Moment of Power

When you decide to accept the changes your colleagues would like to see or explain why you will find it difficult to do so.

14.4 Know when to adapt or innovate

What's the difference? Adaptors prefer to set their problems, however big and complex, into the generally agreed paradigm or model, with a clear aim, using approved method. So, as an outcome of solving problems, they change the paradigm by evolutionary improvements that are careful, safe and efficient. Their weakness is being overcautious when innovation (seen as revolution) is needed.

Innovators are more likely to want to change the model or paradigm in order to solve the problem. This is vital when the current paradigm or accepted way of doing things cannot readily solve the current problem – evolution can take too long and sometimes more risk is acceptable. The innovator's weakness is to doubt the current paradigm too soon, believing that revolutionary innovation is always best.

Being human, of course, we are never one extreme or the other. Adaptors are capable of innovation, and Innovators are capable of adaption. But you and your colleagues have an inbuilt preference for one or the other. The Kirton™ Adaption-Innovation Inventory[5] provides an indication of where people sit on the continuum between the two extremes.

So how does one group regard the others?

- *Adaptors are seen by Innovators as*: sound, conforming, safe, predictable, inflexible, wedded to the system, intolerant of ambiguity.
- *Innovators are seen by Adaptors as*: glamorous, exciting, unsound, impractical, risky, threatening the established system and causing dissonance.

In organizations, Adaptors are essential for on-going functions, but in times of unexpected changes they may have some difficulty moving out of their established role. Innovators are essential in times of change or crisis, but may have trouble applying themselves to on-going organizational demands.

Both are equally important characteristics; one isn't better than the other, they are simply more suited to different times in an organization's life-cycle. But if you and your team lean towards one extreme or the other, there is a danger that you may not give as much attention to either the more radical or less radical options that the problem may warrant. In a team approach to problem solving it is vital for you, as the manager, to ensure that all its diversities of style and capacity collaborate effectively.

Perhaps this is one more facet for you to think about when you next recruit? Don't necessarily select the best person on paper, but try instead to select the individual who will be the best fit for the team's future challenges.

Your Moment of Power

When you seek input to problem solving from those with a completely different approach to your own.

14.5   Recruit the person and not the CV/résumé

Recruiting new people to your team is another one of your most important responsibilities: have you screened for personality; for emotional intelligence; for absent Belbin team-role types in your team; obtained the opinion of others; double-checked the claims made on the CV (many may be fictitious); and personally spoken with two or three people who have worked with this potential new recruit before?

Before making the hiring decision, some managers in some companies even ask the potential workmates of the new recruit for their opinions on the potential new joiner. Although I have never used it – I like the idea.

A cautionary tale. I want you for a moment, to regard yourself as a hunting/shooting/fishing type of person, an alpha male or female. You hold non-PC views, make rude body noises, regularly make inappropriate remarks to the opposite sex, stand with your feet apart, arms crossed in front of you, telling the world your opinion about company performance, world events and sport. Got the image?

Now, a potential recruit with an excellent CV or résumé enters your office and after talking through her professional qualifications, you ask her to tell you a little more about herself as a person. "Well," she says, "I'm a hunting/shooting/fishing type of person, some call me an alpha female. I don't hold with all this political correctness nonsense, I call a spade, a spade. I make rude body noises and make inappropriate remarks to the opposite sex. I stand with my feet apart, arms crossed in front of me, firmly expressing my opinion about company performance, world events and green issues."

Next up, her rival. A quiet, shy male, with an equally impressive CV or résumé, takes his seat opposite you. After talking through his professional qualifications, you ask him to tell you a little more about himself as a person. "There's not much to tell really. I love my job and generally lead a quiet life with my cat, Fluffy. I like reading and for relaxation I enjoy decorating cakes."

Who will you choose? I have told this imaginary story many times. Why? Because most people demonstrate a tendency to recruit in their own image, and you should guard against it. You know that you're good at your job, so someone exactly like you will be too, right? Well, possibly. Possibly not.

I remember that on one occasion, after interviewing three short-listed candidates, I turned to my HR manager and said, "John obviously." "Absolutely not," he replied, "it must be Mick." We spent the next hour justifying our preferences to each other, and in that process I was persuaded to change my mind. I went with Mick and he became a star in my organization.

You may consider having one or two people with you when you next recruit.

Recruit the person and not the CV/résumé.[6]

Your Moment of Power

When you refuse to be dazzled by the candidate's similarities to you and their technical qualifications, and instead focus on his or her character and credentials.

THEIR REACTIONS

15.1 Don't improve the plan if it loses their commitment

When you are asked to critique a piece of work or a plan, either written or verbal, I suspect that there is a strong tendency for you to feel the need to add value. After all, you are older and wiser! You make a suggestion here and another there; you genuinely want to improve the plan and demonstrate both your experience and expertise.

But, and yes it's a very big but, if the changes you suggest are anything but very minor, you run the risk of changing "their plan" to "your plan". As a result, the ownership and pride your team members felt in their work before your contributions may have reduced, or worse, evaporated all together. If the changes are very minor, do you really need to make them at all?

A plan is usually a lot easier to construct than it is to execute. "Here is our plan to reduce the Government's debt over the medium term." Hmm! The execution phase depends largely upon the commitment and passion of those responsible for the implementation. So, are they more likely or less likely to commit fervently to it after you have made some amendments?

Be careful. In some circumstances it may be better to let an imperfect plan be pursued passionately, than try to improve it and, in that process, destroy the motivation and commitment to it.

But if your input is really necessary, then offer it quickly. Otherwise you will become the gating factor. Progress will be delayed until you respond, and by delaying a particular decision you are depriving your colleagues of a feeling of satisfaction and pride in their day's work.

Your people are amazingly resilient, but think about the production potential if, with your help, they did more, achieved more? Liberate your people. Let them get on with their day and make the progress they have targeted.

Your Moment of Power

When you allow people to implement their plan (however imperfect) rather than your plan.

15.2 Let your people see the end results of their efforts

I've often heard the phrase "you do your job and let me worry about the bigger picture" and it always disappoints me. The majority of your people don't like to be pigeon-holed and restricted in their thinking. Most enjoy seeing more than just a glimpse of the bigger picture too, and I bet that some of your objectives actually require your team to see the bigger picture. They want to understand how the entire organization delivers benefits and want to be a part of it; they want to feel that they have made a contribution, however small, to the greater good. The alternative is an "us and them", "workers" and "management" environment.

If managers force employees to focus narrowly on their world, responsibility for team or even company-wide performance becomes someone else's responsibility. It gets delegated upwards. The workers become detached; commitment and motivation diminishes.

If it is at all possible, let your team see first-hand the results of their contributions. If your factory makes nuts and bolts for the Boeing 787, why not arrange to take a tour of the plane when it's in the hangar? The big picture can be a powerful motivator.

Your Moment of Power

When you inspire your people by showing them the end results of their hard labours.

15.3 Watch out for signs of stress

Stress can be a killer if very high levels are endured over long periods. But high levels of temporary stress can prove to be the road to greater fulfilment and increased confidence; imagine your first parachute jump. "I never thought I would be able to do that! It was brilliant!" Stress can be good in the very short term but is proven to be extremely debilitating if endured at high levels in the longer term.[1]

So, let's be clear what we mean by stress. It is defined as mental or emotional tension: strain.

Most people are under stress, most of the time. What should concern effective managers searching for the extra 1% is that the level of stress and the duration and the threshold at which stress becomes debilitating differs dramatically between individuals. It can even vary widely for one individual, more or less in line with the variation in their base state of mind.

Your job as a manager is to watch closely for signs of excessive stress in your people. So, what are those signs? Here are some to watch for:

- Change of personality.
- Loss of concentration.
- Change of habits.
- Lethargy, diffidence.
- Changes in bearing and demeanour.
- Irritability.
- Mood swings.
- Excess concentration on relatively unimportant elements.
- Temper outbursts.
- Drinking more.
- Smoking more.
- Substance abuse.
- Unexplained absences.

Tragically, over the past few years there have been a number of well-publicized suicides at work because these symptoms were not spotted or dealt with. Two global companies immediately spring to mind. Thankfully, however, these are very rare.

So, for each of your team members, you need to consider two aspects of stress management:

How much stress are they under?   Low/Medium/High

For how long have they endured it?   Short/Medium/Long

There is not much you can do to prevent an individual's self-perceived level of stress as it is a very personal thing. But it is your duty to help your people manage stressful situations more effectively and reduce the impact of stress on their health.

If you become concerned about one individual in particular, then the first step is to talk with them privately and confidentially about it. Be prepared for them to deny that they show symptoms – many regard admitting it as a weakness and feel that the condition will affect their prospects within the company. You need to reassure them that it won't!

Persevere. Ask them to identify the triggers that increase stress to high levels for them; both people and situations. And then ask them to try and put the list in priority order for you. Be prepared for you to be the number one reason!

Then suggest that they seek either professional help from their doctor or help themselves by studying coping mechanisms on the internet. Ask them to identify ways of managing the stress more effectively and give you an occasional update on their discoveries. Again, reassure them – "Hey, you're not alone. We all suffer from severe stress at one time or another. Don't worry."

Now, look in the mirror. How would you assess your own levels of stress right now? For how long has it been this way? Treat yourself as you would one of your staff members. Search the internet for coping mechanisms and stress relieving techniques.

Your Moment of Power

When you take stress seriously and talk openly about it with your people.

THEIR MOTIVATIONS

16.1 Prioritize team awards over individual recognition

I have noticed that many hotels and hospitals offer an "Employee Hall of Fame", a wall of smiling employee faces, normally located in a corridor with high footfall. I've seen similar photo walls in office reception areas as well.

Maybe your organization has a similar scheme. After all, recognizing and acknowledging the contribution of junior staff should be a motivational thing to do, shouldn't it? As with many company schemes, the answer is both yes and no.

While it can be operated fairly, you should think really hard before replicating something like this. Why? Because any device, prize, recognition or award that creates winners also, by definition, creates many more losers in the same process.

Many of those who fail to get recognized may feel hard done by. "It's not fair that John got the recognition, he was out for most of the time." You may hurt the feelings of those not recognized – unintentionally I know, but de-motivational all the same.

How often do you see the same person highlighted every month? Rarely, even though they may deserve it. The whole process then becomes devalued – it becomes Buggin's turn. Meaningless and divisive.

If you really want the team to work together, then create a team-based award. A meal at a restaurant for example. Or something even simpler and less expensive – cake or chocolate for all those involved in a positive result.

So lose those employee of the month honours and get thinking along these lines:

> *"Thank you all for your hard work these past few weeks – output has been fantastic. So you can either arrive one hour late or leave one hour early in the next few days so that you can do something for yourself that you have been meaning to do for a while. Just let me know when you'd like to take the extra hour."*

Now that's what I call management.

Your Moment of Power

When you take every opportunity to build a greater sense of community by thanking the group as a whole for the contributions they make to the bigger picture.

16.2   Don't treat people the way you wish to be treated

You must not assume that other people are just like you. They're not!

Instead treat people the way they wish to be treated.

It could be a lot different.

Which means that "Treating others as you yourself wish to be treated" is wrong!

So for example, imagine if someone has done a spectacularly good job and, ignoring the advice given in the previous sub-section, you want to recognize them at a big company gathering. Check with them first. They may not want the public adulation you so crave, and instead fear acute embarrassment. Some people don't like the limelight. If you were fired, you may be self-sufficient and not want the outplacement service, but someone you're firing might.

Treat your people the way *they* wish to be treated.

You will be rewarded if, for example, your circumstances allow you to be flexible with start and finish times. Some people work far better in the afternoons than in the mornings and vice versa. Some people need to drop off or pick up their children from school. You may find that, given the freedom to self-manage, your people might actually get the same or more work done in shorter time periods than previously.

It's also important to understand that other people don't think like you do. They think like they do.

You may be very good at understanding detail or seeing the big picture or both, but the chances of your individual people viewing their work and the team goals the same way as you do are extremely slim.

Management versus the Unions. "Can't they see how damaging this will be to the company?" vs "Can't they see how their proposals will result in an unacceptable lowering of our members' living standards?"

The way that you see a problem or opportunity will not be the same way as your people view it. Therefore, their sense of importance or urgency will not match yours. This means that you will get rewarded for trying seriously to see the world as your people do.

If you have a greater understanding of their individual worlds then you will have a greater success with initiatives for the extra 1%; but, I do understand that in some cultures it is almost impossible to find out how others are really thinking.

Your Moment of Power

When you do what each of your individual people believe and feel is right for them, instead of doing what you think is right for them.

16.3   Rethink the idea of incentives

Most people want to do the right thing and they shouldn't need incentives to do it.

Offering an individual or group extra money for hitting an arbitrary target may unwittingly cause behaviours to change for the worse.[1]

And even targets that don't carry a financial reward need very careful handling. An example. A team handling customers may get complaints, by letter, by email or by phone. Some companies I know have, in the past, targeted a reduction in the numbers of complaints and offered incentives to their staff. Sounds a reasonable target, doesn't it? Let's identify the root causes of the complaints and correct them. Great!

But the staff will naturally try to deliver the outcome targeted, thereby making their boss happy. Now, unlike before, there is a risk that those people will not record every complaint as they should. Why? Because, aware that fewer complaints are the target, they will genuinely ask themselves if that last call was really a complaint, or was it just bringing a particular weakness in the system to the company's attention. "I don't think that was a genuine complaint, more of a helpful suggestion." The people are not trying to deceive or falsify. No. They are trying to hit your arbitrary target, and they probably would have done so anyway, even without the "incentive".

So, target hit, everyone wins, yes? No. Because the managers are now less aware of the company's shortcomings. If identifying the root causes of complaints was the real objective, then the company would have been in a better position if *an increase* in the number of complaints was targeted.

I've also learned that in some companies where staff operate in a hazardous environment or a potentially dangerous one, incentives have been given for the reporting of hazards or procedures not being followed properly. I believe instead that people should do the right thing or face a reprimand.

So, unless the personalities of your people put "money" at the centre of their decision making (and some sales people do), spend as much time as necessary convincing people of the right-ness of the proposed course of action. Once convinced, most people will do the right thing anyway, irrespective of any incentive. After all we rarely, if ever, drive through a red light, even if there is no one around to catch us at three in the morning. The reason is that we agree with the "correctness" of this rule on safety grounds.

But let's suppose that you do want a bit of extra insurance that things will go well. What could work if money doesn't? If you want universal commitment, why not simply try to introduce an element of fun and involve everyone.

Your Moment of Power

When you spend time convincing your people of the right-ness of the targets and goals instead of offering a quick reward.

16.4 Give more than money

Money is not the only motivator. Instead, use every opportunity to personally display your appreciation, trust or confidence in good employees. It costs nothing but a little time, personal effort and awareness to minimize the destructive "them and us" culture. Everyone in your team is important, and each individual should be valued as such. A £15k company car left unused in the car park would soon provoke an adverse staff reaction, but so often front-line employees can easily just be left to get on with it for months at a time without recognition, stimulation or perform-ance evaluation (with appropriate feedback).

Assuming that people can be relied upon to work better with more money is an easy mistake to make. Yes, it's quick and easy, but what people really want, provided that their pay package is fair and in line with their effort, is your time and attention. It's not an easy lesson to learn – but well worth the effort!

But giving too much of your time and attention to perhaps one or two people, instead of sharing it more equally, may give rise to the issue of favouritism. If I asked each of your team individu-ally who was your favourite person – do you think they would be able to tell me? Do you transmit your favouritism by paying some individuals more attention than others? Do you seek the opinions of some of your team and ignore the opinions of others? If yes, did you set out to do so, or has this situation developed over time and almost by accident?

I refer to this because fairness is extremely important for everyone that works for you. People will put up with a lot of things, providing they believe they are treated fairly. Whether you think it's fair is irrelevant – they must think it's fair.

Here is an example. One very good investment banker I know told me of his annual bonus one January a few years ago and I was astonished, as you would be, by the hundreds of thousands mentioned. "That's good, I said, are you pleased?" "No I'm not," he replied. "It's not fair – Jack got a lot more and that's not right." Fairness was more important in this situation than the actual amount of bonus. So his manager achieved the impossible – demotivating this particular staff member with a six-figure bonus. Brilliant!

Without showing favouritism, spend a bit more time with your stars than with your weakest performers. Sounds counter-intuitive at first, but the chances are your stars will be able to increase their output faster than those of more modest ambitions and capabilities. If you find that you are spending a dis-proportionately high amount of time with your weakest, you will need to think seriously about replacing them, and sooner rather than later.

Don't let your weakest hold you back from achieving the extra 1%.

Your Moment of Power

When your people feel that they are rewarded fairly both with money and your attention when compared to their colleagues.

16.5 Know when it's time for the stick!

So having chosen your incentives, or carrots, carefully, you discover that some people are not the vegetarians you thought they were and are not making the changes you desire, or not making them fast enough. What next?

Time to put down the carrot and pick up the stick. At this point, many managers that I have known have resorted to raising their voices, shouting even, about the perceived lack of self-motivation. So who suffers most in this situation? The manager, because they have displayed some very unattractive qualities, and who would want to work their heart out for someone who displays unattractive qualities?

Bawling someone out is wrong, disrespectful and largely ineffective. Just imagine your emotions and what you would be thinking of if you had just been bawled out. Anger, perhaps embarrassment, thoughts of invoking the grievance procedure, lodging a formal complaint, resigning? Little room left for refocusing on the task in hand and making more progress.

So what should you do?

In private, give voice to your disappointment and ask for an explanation:

> "John, you are an important member of the team, and I think you have let yourself down with regard to Project X. I had thought that you would have made more progress by now. Can you help me to understand what's going on?"

Ask them how they feel about their achievements and performance.

If, after listening to the answers, you decide on some corrective action, what are your options? How about asking them?

"How would you like to make up for your behaviour/performance?" "What would you do in my position faced with this level of performance?"

Sometimes you can use the stick without saying anything at all. Imagine that you have arranged for your team to visit another site and told your staff that the bus will leave at 1100 hrs. You then instruct the driver to depart at precisely 1100 hrs and not one minute past. Those not on board (there are always latecomers) are left to find the way themselves at their expense. You've made the point.

Your Moment of Power

When your team accepts that there will be consequences from a lack of focus on the achievement of maximum output, which are fair, proportionate and delivered privately without anger.

THEIR TALENTS

17.1 Recognize their number one talent

You have immensely talented people; and I'm not only describing work-related technical expertise, but also those softer skills, like a sense of humour or thoughtfulness. Using the table below, record the names of your people and what you believe to be their number one talent.

Name	Number 1 Talent

You may consider asking those individuals if you are correct in your assessment.

Then ask yourself whether the job they are doing leverages those particular talents. You may have the right people on the team, but do you have them in the right seats for maximum production? Could you get an extra 1% by making minor adjustments to roles and responsibilities?

You can throw away most corporate job descriptions because they fail to identify and leverage the talents and skills of the individuals who hold the jobs. They are usually designed for the position and not the person. Unless yours are any different, they may never exploit the experience and talents of a specific individual. They tend to remain the same, irrespective of who holds the position. Ridiculous!

An example: a generic job description may not include the need for the position holder to be a good presenter, but the actual person holding the job may be a natural showman. As an excellent boss, you'd leverage that talent for the wider good wouldn't you? So consider re-writing your job descriptions, acknowledging the two or three key strengths of each individual.

The best managers make their people feel special.

Your Moment of Power

When you re-write the job description of each of your people in such a way as to tap into their natural talents.

17.2 Let your people make mistakes!

People learn most from making mistakes. I certainly did.

In Chapter 8 I suggested that in some circumstances, "doing things" can be more beneficial than lengthy analysis and planning, even if you do the wrong thing and then have to correct it. I also stated in the same chapter that if you move from red to green and then to amber, then it's not too much of a stretch to imagine that mistakes will occur.

What this entails, of course, is that you may need to let your people make mistakes too, so that they learn and gain vital experience. This may become a very challenging test for you if you can foresee the mistakes that will be made. Will you let them make the foreseeable mistake? I know one recently promoted senior manager who, being able to foresee many of these occasions, spends about one third of his day putting insurances and fall-back positions into place, so that if or when the mistake occurs, it doesn't affect the team's output too significantly. This means that the team is learning and developing, and gradually producing more.

However, in those circumstances, you will need to differentiate clearly between failure and blame. If a particular course of action fails after all of the risks were identified and mitigated, then blame would not be appropriate; but if one high risk could or should have been identified, and wasn't, then it becomes necessary to criticize the performance and not the person. In private of course. Unfortunately, there exists a strong blame culture in many organizations. It's certainly true in different sports. You hear the phrase, "It was his fault/It was her fault" all too often. Clearly differentiate between the person and their performance.

One debriefing technique I recommend is the STAR debriefing model.

- **S**ituation.
- **T**ask.
- **A**ction.
- **R**esult.

Remember that the focus is on the activity and not on the person.

So, if you compare the following examples of an UNSTAR debrief with its STAR opposite, you'll be able to spot the difference in result/effect:

UNSTAR: *"You did a poor job on that project, John."*

STAR: *"John, I was a bit disappointed with your performance on the XYZ Project. As you know, we were working under a very tight deadline. I was counting on you to complete the data analysis on Task B, as per our project meetings. Because you didn't communicate with me or give me a heads-up that you were not going to meet the deadline, I was unaware until the last minute that Task B would not be complete and that did put me in an awkward spot and almost caused the project to be canceled completely. That cannot happen again. As I see it . . ."*

- *Situation:* "John, I was a bit disappointed with your performance on the XYZ Project. As you know, we were working under a very tight deadline."
- *Task:* "I was counting on you to complete the data analysis on Task B, as per our project meetings."
- *Action:* "Because you didn't communicate with me or give me a heads-up that you were not going to meet the deadline."
- *Result:* "I was unaware until the last minute that Task B would not be complete and that did put me in an awkward

spot and almost caused the project to be canceled
completely."

Your Moment of Power

When you let your people make mistakes but then use the
STAR debrief model naturally and without prior thought.

17.3   Ask, don't tell!

Contrast the following two utterances of someone tempted to switch employer in order to get a higher-level job:

Statement: "I need to be given higher-level work soon or I will have to look around for other opportunities."

with

Question: "If you were in my shoes, how long would you wait before seeking new horizons?"

Actually asking the question: "What would you do in my position?" is a very useful way of trying to bridge gaps in attitude or understanding.

And when seeking information or feedback, instead of asking "How's the project going, Betty?" you may consider, "Betty, what's the biggest frustration you have with the project?" or "What's your biggest concern about meeting the deadline for the project?"

If someone asks you a question during a formal presentation that you had planned to address later in the same presentation, I recommend you consider addressing it immediately, saying "Good question – let me answer that right now" and flip forward through your material to the relevant section. The alternative, and I have many times in the past been guilty of saying "Can I ask you to hold that question for a little later" is for me (with the benefit of hindsight), a little disrespectful.

If the same people are often asking you the same or similar questions, take time out to think about why that might be. Possible reasons include:

- They are uncertain of their authority levels.
- They lack confidence with a particular element of the job.

- They need regular reassurance.
- Their work demands a higher level of skill or competency than they possess.
- They are ingratiating themselves.

Addressing the issue quickly, perhaps with questions of your own, will minimize the time they steal from you, affording you more time to think and manage.

Your Moment of Power

When the power and scope of your question forces people to stop and complete a fundamental reappraisal of the situation.

17.4   Delegate more often as a sign of the trust you have in others!

Delegation is the hottest and most pressing subject for managers that I have come across. Ever! Most managers don't think they delegate well or delegate enough.

They say things like, "I'm the most qualified and knowledgeable person for this task," "If I delegate it then I'll spend more time briefing the task than it would take me to do it," "I've more experience and I get paid the most, so I should do it."

But we also know that efficient delegation helps us to manage our time more effectively and wisely. Managing, not operating. So, you decide to listen to your own advice and delegate more. What is the first question that you need to answer? I suggest it's this: "What are the operational activities or things that I do best." Why? Because I ask you to consider delegating these activities first. The chances are that they include the very same things that got you promoted to manager in the first place. If you don't make a conscious effort to forego them, however, the risk is that you may continue to do too much operating and not enough managing.

In addition you may wish to consider the following:

- Ensure that the delegatee has the skills and competencies to do the job well.
- Seek their agreement that they are willing to do the work, which is usually in addition to their normal work.
- Delegate important work as well as the menial. Avoid delegating most of the menial to one person and all of the important work to someone else. Balance carefully.

- Tell them that you trust them to get the job done properly and within the time constraints. It gives their confidence a boost.
- Tell them how you would normally do the work, but give them license to adopt their own method if they would prefer.
- Make sure they have enough resource and time to do the job properly.
- Tell them that you are always available to them, providing out of hours numbers if appropriate. "Don't hesitate to call me anytime if you have any questions or concerns."
- Make sure you respond to any of their enquiries quickly.
- Before shaking hands with them and wishing them luck, ask them to tell you in their words what they think they have agreed. It's your last opportunity to double-check their understanding.

Many people enjoy additional responsibility – but not all. Before handing out more of it, you may want to make sure that those to whom you have delegated feel they have the confidence to handle it.

Your Moment of Power

When the work that you delegate demonstrates how much you trust your people to shoulder greater responsibility.

THEIR BEHAVIOURS

18.1 Be on your guard for monkeys!

Sometimes, your people will try to delegate upwards to you! You may have heard the phase "To get the monkey off my shoulder". Translated, this means that one of your people has a problem, issue or challenge and they are unsure of how to proceed and really want you to make the decision and take responsibility for implementing it away from them so it's not their problem anymore, it's yours. It's not their monkey, it's your monkey!

When I was working in London, one of my colleagues had a fantastic way of dealing with these situations. He sat in what can only be described as a sterile office. There were no pictures or paintings, no photographs or certificates, nothing to show that the office was even occupied. On his desk was a telephone and a computer. That's all. No in-tray, out-tray, no papers, trade periodicals – nothing. When his people came to see him to get him to take ownership of a particular problem, or move the monkey from their shoulder onto his, he approached the meeting as follows:

1. He would take one sheet of A4 from one drawer and a pencil from another.
2. He would ask for a statement of the problem or issue. He would record every detail of it onto the A4 sheet. He

would ask many probing questions to ensure his complete understanding of the issue.

3. He would ask for options on how to solve the issue or address the problem. He would try to get as many options as possible recorded, pressing the person sitting opposite to think hard and imaginatively. On occasions he would ask the person to go away and come back when they had thought of more options before continuing.

4. He would ask the person for their recommendation, and then ask them to justify it. He would ask for reasons why the other options should be rejected, recording those as well.

5. He then asked what, if he agreed with the recommendation, would be the next two or three actions. He recorded those.

6. He then replayed everything he had heard, reading from his notes, just as a judge would when summing up. He asked if there was anything more that should be discussed.

7. Without anything further, he stated his agreement with the proposed course of action, took a copy of his notes and handed the original to his visitor. "OK. I agree with your recommendation and your course of action. Go ahead. Let me know how you get on."

The visitor had tried to shift the monkey from their own shoulder onto the manager's. The visitor left the office with the monkey still on his or her own shoulder, but a lot more confident and content, having been forced to think through the issue in detail and to consider alternatives. There was no resentment. His people really appreciated the process.

Say "No" to the monkey.

Your Moment of Power

When your ultra-sensitive radar detects a monkey on the horizon and you help your people to accept ownership by forcing them to understand and assess alternative courses of action.

18.2 Don't ask for permission, ask for forgiveness

Some actions at work are urgent and cannot wait for higher-level authority. No problem if they align with company policy. But others, which you genuinely believe are necessary and in the company's best interests, may not align with normal company policy or guidelines. If they are still just as time sensitive, what do you do?

You should consider doing what you think is right. And communicate your actions immediately, so that those higher up are not caught out unexpectedly.

I remember, during civil unrest in a Mediterranean country, that a bus carrying perhaps a couple of dozen people was stopped by protesters and the passengers became very fearful. Luckily the driver forced his way through the crowd. One of the passengers was asked later, what would have happened if the driver had not acted as he did? The passenger replied that he would have pulled the driver from his seat and driven the bus himself, "But do you have a licence?" asked the journalist. Some people!

Now, imagine that one of your people is unintentionally put into the same awkward position. How will you respond? Will you assume accountability for their actions, even though they may have exceeded their authority levels, and tell your boss that you believe they did the right thing in the circumstances? Or, by contrast, will you condemn them to your boss and discipline them?

Your Moment of Power

When you stand up for your people when they need it most even if it means that you or they take a considered decision that potentially runs counter to stated company policy.

18.3 Just say "no" to micromanagement

Micromanagement of your staff is a brilliant, if annoying and demotivating, example of a bad management habit borne out of one of these three reasons:

- You don't trust the employee to get the job done to the standard or timeline that you require.
- You are frightened that because your own boss is a micromanager, requests for an excessive number of progress reports will be made, and you want to be seen as on top of things.
- Or a combination of both of the above.

It can be very disheartening and demoralizing for anyone on your team if you brief them to undertake a certain course of action or achieve a specific objective and then ask for frequent updates, or interrupt their work (in person, telephone or email) to check on progress. Stop it! Instead, let them get on with it.

But what if it's a critical piece of work and as the senior manager in charge you're really nervous? If that's the case then tell your team members, firmly, how important their work is and that you are very nervous and that you want to know immediately if things start to go even slightly awry. Make sure they understand that if they detect a potential problem, you should be notified immediately and that waiting and hoping that things will improve is not acceptable to you.

But what if your boss is a micromanager and is constantly demanding updates to your activities and outputs – contacting you several times a day? Disappointingly, bad behaviour lower down the management ladder often replicates behaviour from higher up.

But you will only change the behaviour of your boss if you first change yours. You have to be your boss's "mini me". By that I mean don't wait for him or her to contact you for updates, get on the front foot and send them regular updates without being asked and go for more detail than they have requested. Overload them with data. For you this might be very tiresome, but after a while (days, weeks or even months), I am hoping that they will have learned to trust you with your management tasks and you both agree to a modified reporting model which is more rewarding.

Your Moment of Power

When you stop yourself from asking a micromanaging question and instead let the person you have asked to do the job get on with their work.

18.4 "I feel that . . ."

This is a very important phrase. For you and for your people.

Let's compare the following two statements. If you said "You don't trust me," it allows the other person to come back with "Of course I do," or "It's not a matter of trust" and then the conversation continues with both parties trying to counter the other's arguments. But if you said, "I feel that you don't trust me," contradiction is impossible because you are stating your true feelings. The other person is more likely to come back with "Why do you say that?" I suggest that this technique can lead to a more productive conversation.

You can use this prefix to discuss your deepest concerns with your boss, your peer group and your staff. You can use it at work and away from work.

- "I feel disappointed . . ."
- "I feel sad . . ."
- "I feel disillusioned . . ."
- "I feel threatened . . ."
- "I feel concerned . . ."
- "I feel overworked . . ."
- "I feel under pressure . . ."

Articulate your concerns early, after a short period of reflection. Once you have decided to call a meeting, then first thing the next day, arrange it or fix a time to speak with the other party.

Similarly, if you feel great, empowered, positive, upbeat, which I am sure you do for most of the time, then let others know how you feel.

- "I feel great today!"
- "I feel that John is coming around to our way of thinking."
- "I feel on top of the world."
- "I feel we're getting somewhere."

Encourage your people to share with you their true feelings, it can be a very good way to identify frustrations that could possibly be overcome and contribute to the extra 1%. But it's not easy; you will have needed to have built a high level of mutual trust for them to share their innermost thoughts with you.

Your Moment of Power

When you have built a level of trust between you and your people so that they feel comfortable telling you their true feelings.

THEIR CAREER CHANGES

19.1   Deal with difficult people

In every team there is always one person, or occasionally two, that need a little more careful handling than the others. You may even classify some of these people as "difficult", even though others may not.

And that brings us to the heart of the matter. You may be the problem in this relationship, far more than the person you classify as "difficult". Examine your own emotions and feelings first. Why have you classified them as difficult? Do they have more knowledge, qualifications, social power, status, physical attractiveness, admirers than you? Are their frustrations taken out on you, as their manager?

After examining your feelings, I ask you to consider sharing your feelings with the other person.

In a private conversation admit your feelings with:

> *"I feel that our relationship could be improved"* or *"I would like our working relationship to improve".*

Explain why you feel the way you do. Seek their thoughts and feelings. Maybe there is something that one of you does, or doesn't do, that particularly annoys the other. Try to bottom it out. And call it earlier rather than later.

> ### *Your* Moment of Power
>
> When you understand that, with the right handling, sometimes the most difficult people can make the greatest contributions.

19.2 Consider if a change of culture is needed

I have heard the phrase "We have to change the culture around here" all too often. If you find yourself saying the same thing, and have decided to do something about it, then be warned; it will take a long time and involve everyone in the organization, mainly senior and middle managers.

The culture of an organization is set at the very top. So that's where the change will need to happen first. Experience has shown that the most senior are the hardest to change! So, before starting down this road ask yourself this question:

If your organization or team has performed consistently in the upper quartile of its sector for many years, it will have developed a culture that people are drawn towards, be it ruthless or family friendly, and it would be foolish to change it. If, however, your organization is either slipping down the rankings or has performed consistently in the lowest quartile, then a culture change should be properly evaluated.[1]

So, how would you describe the culture in your team? How do your team describe the culture? Are they the same? Is the culture one that you have developed or one that you have inherited? Is it a culture that attracts applicants? Do you think the culture is appropriate for the challenges that lie ahead? Are there habits that you would like to change? Tread carefully and take advice.

Your Moment of Power

When you acknowledge that a change of culture is necessary in order to create and maintain a high achievement culture.

19.3   Accept that sometimes they have to go

One of the hardest things to do as a manager is to let go of an underperforming employee. It's sometimes perceived as an admission that you made a selection mistake or that your ability to get the best from your people is not quite as strong as you may have thought.

But you can rarely fire someone who is ill-suited to a task or company culture too soon. Indeed, by waiting too long you hurt both your company and the individual's prospects of finding better-suited employment. For those who you ask to change career course, you should offer to pay for a support mechanism in the form of an outplacement service or counsellor.

If you do have to fire someone because their performance or attitude is not up to scratch, the remainder of your team will bear close witness to your words and deeds. The firing may not be a surprise to them, but it may still shock them.

When the person in question has departed, you need to call your team together and explain your actions and the reasons behind them. Why? Because they will all have two questions burning brightly in their minds, although they may not put them into words. "Why him or her?" and "Why now?" The person you fired didn't become a bad person overnight, and some of your team may remain friends with them long after they have left.

When inheriting a new team – give everyone a couple of months to assess their capabilities and output potential – but don't be afraid to fire those who you assess to be unlikely to make much of a contribution to your teams' future efforts. When making the assessment you may wish to consider MBTI, 360°, Belbin, LDQ etc. (see Chapters 13 and 14).

Ensure that you follow company protocol and local law and, through your words and deeds, aim for your remaining people to acknowledge that you did it professionally and with care and sensitivity.

Your Moment of Power

When you finally decide, after much soul-searching, to upgrade your team; and steel yourself to tell one of your colleagues, friends even, that they will need to find alternative employment.

19.4 Accept when it's time for you to move on

Success in your current role will lead to other opportunities, and you will need to hand over the reins to your successor at some point. So, have you identified the person who can take over your role when you move on to greater things?

Failure to plan for your successor can mean a period of short-termism. Temporary managers will not feel that they have the authority to make big changes because they are simply keeping the seat warm for the longer-term successor (Rafael Benitez at Chelsea FC). Contrast Hewlett Packard, who had four chief executives between 2005 and 2011, and interim executive cover between them, with the successful handover at General Electric between Jack Welch and Jeffrey Immelt.

So, who to choose?

Although they may or may not come directly from your team, deciding upon your own replacement is one of your top priorities. If you have not identified a ready replacement, maybe you should add it to your "thinking about" list. You may wish to consult others, including your boss. You may need to recruit. Then, of course, they need to be trained and developed so that they perform just as well, or ideally even better, than you when they take over.

So, what qualities will you be looking for in your potential replacement? Consider the following:

- Carefully define the context in which your replacement will be working and the level of change likely during that person's tenure.
- Are you looking for someone who could be a big picture, strategic thinker during periods of significant

change or someone who loves to work the detail when the work pattern is stable?

- What external challenges will your replacement need to tackle?
- Will the team face cost cutting or a rapid expansion?
- Look inside the organization for likely candidates before looking outside.
- Search for people who display an inner strength of character and a mature attitude.
- And finally, define the narrow technical expertise that will be necessary.

I have a strong belief that a professional, effective manager in one industry can move sideways into a new industry without knowing the absolute detail of the team's work. For example, I believe an effective factory manager may be able to run a hospital; a good sales manager may be able to run an R & D function; a good finance manager may be able to run a production line. For me, the focus should be more on the management competencies and interpersonal skills of the person rather than their technical knowledge. Too often I have found people constrained and limited by too literal an appreciation of their past.

So, who is on your shortlist?

Your Moment of Power

When you accept that you can do no more, leave on your own terms and hand over to someone who shows the promise of being even better then you.

CONCLUSION

The Little Black Book for Managers has revisited scenarios you will have witnessed many times before as a manager or an employee and wondered "Why did that situation or strategy turn out so poorly?" or "What should I or my manager have done instead?" The recommendations provided have drawn upon both personal insight and the latest in academic research. They have offered up useful and practical suggestions for how to seize upon those moments of power in your life as a manager when you *can* actually make a real difference. When your team *can* work up to its full potential and achieve that extra 1% of output or quality that sets you and your team apart.

I've shown you many examples, ideas and ways of thinking and doing that you can follow from principle to execution, by exercising your moments of power. If there is one underlying "truth" that permeates many if not all of the moments of power I have touched upon in this book, it is that they don't necessarily follow from *common intuition* or *ease of execution*. In fact, on the face of it at least, some of the moments of power may seem to fly in the face of intuition and land right smack in the path of most resistance. You know that we, as human beings first with all our differing experiences, contrasting impulses and hard-wiring, can easily be fooled by "received wisdom" and that the truly wise manager who is successful over the long term always strives to do what's best, not what's easiest.

This underlying tenet may mean not relying on your first rush to judgement, no matter how quickly and easily it comes to mind. Yes, there are rules that under normal times allow us to park our brains and merely appeal to them when in difficulty, but there are times so unique that the rules, like the notes on a page for a fine jazz musician, need to be eschewed in favour of the tenor and tone of the moment or the "room".

Your success as a manager hinges on those elements that are under your direct or indirect control. The people and situations described previously obtain whether you are riding an economic wave of prosperity or are in the clutches of a bear market. Free yourself from the paralysis that comes from not being able to accept the cards that have been dealt you and take up the challenge of altering those aspects of your job that can be changed through your own efforts or by marshalling those around you.

We are sometimes afraid to speak our minds and do what is right because of what that might entail, e.g., upset from colleagues, admonitions from the higher-ups, blowback from your employees etc. If as a manager you find yourself in one of those moments, caught between the proverbial rock of a corporate straightjacket and the hard place of risking everything you have personally, then going through our various chapters and noting the many experiences that were not easy, but proved to be right, will reinforce your willpower and perseverance.

The many examples described in *The Little Black Book for Managers* will help you to comply with what is the right and what is the decent thing to do and, more tangibly, you will come to see that your moment of power as a manager is always at hand. The question that rests before you now is whether, the next time that same moment with all its potential power presents itself, *you will choose* to seize it?

So let's finish by restating where we started – in the very first chapter the job of every manager was defined as follows:

- Increase team output in increments of 1%.
- Get the same jobs done to the same or better standards with fewer resources and smaller budgets.
- Make yourself redundant.

To succeed with these three responsibilities and to reinforce your authority, you've been given a rich smorgasbord of ideas and recommendations of how you can leverage your power as a manager. Precisely how successful you will be at exercising this power will depend on how willing you are to modify your habits; adapt your management style; and rethink your approach to situations. I'm not saying that your current habits, style or approach are wrong or inappropriate – simply that an alternative may bring you greater success and richer rewards. Why settle for being 90% effective when 91% is within your grasp? Good luck!

FURTHER READING

FOREWORD

1 To hear Captain Sully: http://www.cbc.ca/whitecoat/blog/2012/11/23/
  sully-sullenberger-lessons-from-my-hero/

CHAPTER 1

1.1 IGNORE YOUR JOB DESCRIPTION

1 Carl Honore (2013), *The Slow Fix: Solve Problems, Work Smarter,
  and Live Better*, Random House, http://www.randomhouse.ca/books/
  212517/the-slow-fix-by-carl-honore

1.2 EMBRACE YOUR ROLE AS A SOCCER COACH AND AN ORCHESTRA CONDUCTOR

2 Investigators have explored how expressive conducting behaviors
  might interact to affect the quality of ensemble expressivity and
  performance. Turns out music students performed music better with
  conductors who displayed expressive gestures compared to unexpressive ones (House, R. E. 1998. "Effects of Expressive and Non-
  Expressive Conducting on the Performance and Attitudes of Advanced
  Instrumentalists." Dissertation Abstracts International, 59A, 4004;
  and Sidoti, V. J. 1990. "The Effects of Expressive and Non-Expressive
  Conducting on the Performance Accuracy of Selected Expressive
  Markings by Individual High School Instrumentalists." Dissertation

Abstracts International, 51, 3270A.). Expressive conductors elicited higher performance ratings from their ensembles than unexpressive conductors, even when the musical excerpts were the same (Morrison, S. J., Price, H. E., Geiger, C., and Cornacchio, R. 2009. "The Effect of Conductor Expressivity on Ensemble Performance Evaluation." *Journal of Research in Music Education*, 57, 37–49. doi:10.1177/0022429409332679). http://jrm.sagepub.com/content/early/2012/10/19/0022429412462580.full.pdf. All research originally discovered in Silvey, Brian A. 2012. "The Role of Conductor Facial Expression in Students' Evaluation of Ensemble Expressivity" *Journal of Research in Music Education* 20(10): 1–11.

3 Academic research shows that managers are crucial in assembling and dynamically evaluating talent, which doesn't necessarily mean hiring the best in each position. There is fit and coordination to consider. Turns out an optimal spread of talent works best (not too big or small a difference between the top and bottom performers on a team works best). See: Rafael Gomez et al. (2011),. "Team Performance and the Optimal Spread of Talent: Evidence from Major League Baseball", *Centrepiece Magazine*. http://cep.lse.ac.uk/pubs/download/cp344.pdf

CHAPTER 2

2.1 LET YOUR PEOPLE SET THEIR OWN OBJECTIVES

1 Worth re-reading Elton Mayo and his legendary work on the Hawthorn Effect. Ref: Richard Gillespie (1991), *Manufacturing Knowledge: A History of the Hawthorne Experiments*, (Cambridge: Cambridge University Press), ISBN 0-521-40358-8.

2.2 TRY NOT TO SET TARGETS

2 Think of Steven Kerr's famous line (which was also his *Harvard Business Review* article title) "On the Folly of Rewarding A, While Hoping for B", Ref: http://www.ou.edu/russell/UGcomp/Kerr.pdf

2.3 IDENTIFY PERFORMANCE POTENTIAL

3 Laurence J. Peter, *The Peter Principle: Why Things Always Go Wrong*, (New York: William Morrow and Company), ISBN 0-688-27544-3. OCLC 1038496/ Ed Lazear paper "The Peter Principle: Promotions and Declining Productivity": http://www-siepr.stanford.edu/Papers/pdf/00-04.pdf

CHAPTER 3

3.1 HAVE UP-TO-DATE PERFORMANCE STATISTICS AT YOUR FINGERTIPS

1 The Pareto Principle was actually coined by Joseph Moses Juran, a quality control engineer who stumbled across the work of economist Vilfredo Pareto in the 1940s and began to apply the Pareto principle to quality issues (for example, 80% of a problem is caused by 20% of the causes). This is also known as "the vital few and the trivial many". In later years, Juran preferred "the vital few and the useful many" to signal the remaining 80% of the causes should not be totally ignored. When he began his career in the 1920s, the principal focus in quality management was on the quality of the end, or finished, product. The tools used were from the Bell system of acceptance sampling, inspection plans, and control charts. The ideas of Frederick Winslow Taylor dominated. In keeping with the orientation of this book, Juran added the human dimension to quality management. He pushed for the education and training of managers. For Juran, human relations problems were the ones to isolate. Resistance to change – or, in his terms, cultural resistance – was the root cause of quality issues.

2 R. Koch (2004), *Living the 80/20 Way: Work Less, Worry Less, Succeed More, Enjoy More*, (London: Nicholas Brealey Publishing), ISBN 1-85788-331-4.

3.2 DRAW AN ACTIVITY TREE

3 To find out more about activity trees and their use in activity based costing, go first to: http://www.economist.com/node/13933812

3.3 DON'T SHY AWAY FROM MAKING OR RECOMMENDING BIG INVESTMENTS

4 Tracy Kidder (2000), *The Soul of a New Machine*, (Back Bay Books), ISBN 0-316-49197-7.

Originally written in 1981, the work environment described in Tracy Kidder's book may be in evidence at Google, but still is in many ways the opposite of traditional management. Instead of top-down management, many of the innovations are started at the grassroots level. Instead of management having to coerce workers to work harder, the engineers volunteer to complete the project on time. Why? Senior management learns that people will give their best when the work itself is challenging and rewarding. Many of the engineers state that, "They don't work for the money", meaning they work for the challenge of inventing and creating. The motivational system is akin to the game of pinball, the analogy that if you win this round, you get to play the game again; that is, build the next generation of computers.

3.4 PREPARE FOR THE POSSIBILITY THAT EVERY ACTION YOU TAKE, MAY INADVERTENTLY CREATE AN EQUAL AND OPPOSITE REACTION

5 This is also known as the law of unintended causes and has a large and long history in the social sciences. It could be said to go back to the writings of English philosopher John Locke who, in the late seventeenth century, opposed legislation limiting the rate of interest not because he was worried about the lenders making less profit, but because he was worried about the unintended shortfall in available credit available to borrowers in true need.

Robert K. Merton (1976), *Sociological Ambivalence and Other Essays*, (New York: Free Press). The first modern and complete analysis of the concept of unintended consequences was published in 1936 by the American sociologist Robert K. Merton. In an influential article titled "The Unanticipated Consequences of Purposive Social Action", Merton identified five sources of unanticipated consequences. The first two – and the most pervasive – were "ignorance" and "error".

CHAPTER 4

4.1 CREATE STICKY HEADLINE MESSAGES

1 In a recent book by Alain de Botton, an inspired case is made for taking the best bits of religion, even if you're an atheist, which means taking advantage of the way religion has always dramatized (either orally or visually) their ideas and lessons, and indeed how repetition is key to making things "stick" in the minds of the congregation.
Alain de Botton (2011), *Religion for Atheists: A Non-believer's Guide to the Uses of Religion* (London: Pantheon).

4.2 CHANGE BEHAVIOURS

2 Well almost every government. Recently the Conservative government of Canada has increased party member contributions and rolled back pensions payout for Members of Parliament. It then proceeded to impose concessions on federal government employees.

4.3 DON'T UNDERESTIMATE THE COSTS OR TIMESCALES OF ANY CHANGES

3 In academic terms this is sometimes known as the Winner's Curse, the problem that befalls companies always performing at a high level, which adjusts market expectations unduly upwards, making even the slightest downward deviation punishable with strong negative over-reactions. Best to manage expectations and not play up success during good times in order to salvage reputational currency during bad times.
Richard H. Thaler (1988), Anomalies: The Winner's Curse, *Journal of Economic Perspectives* 2 (1), 191–202, JSTOR 194275.

CHAPTER 5

5.1 INSPIRE THEM!

1 Marcus Buckingham and Curt Coffman offer a supporting and brilliant explanation of the difference between the duties of a manager and the duties of a leader in their book *First Break All The Rules*, ©Gallup Organization.

CHAPTER 6

6.2 PROTECT YOURSELF AGAINST TIME STEALERS

1 This is backed up by Paul Hammerness and Margaret Moore who, in a 2011 *Harvard Business Review* article, show that while stopping to answer a barrage of emails when working on another task, may help us check off more things on our to-do lists, it also makes us more prone to making mistakes, more likely to miss important information and cues, and less likely to retain information in working memory, which impairs problem solving and creativity.

6.4 INFECT EVERYONE AROUND YOU WITH YOUR UPBEAT MOOD AND POSITIVE ATTITUDE

2 Researchers from Harvard Medical School and the University of California, San Diego have found that "happiness" is not the result solely of a cloistered journey filled with individually-tailored self-help techniques. Happiness is also a collective phenomenon that spreads through social networks like an emotional contagion. In a study that looked at the happiness of nearly 5000 individuals over a period of 20 years, researchers found that when an individual becomes happy, the network effect can be measured up to three degrees. One person's happiness triggers a chain reaction that benefits not only their friends, but their friends' friends, and their friends' friends' friends. The effect lasts for up to one year. James H. Fowler, Nicholas A. Christakis (2008), Dynamic Spread of Happiness in a Large Social Network: Longitudinal Analysis Over 20 Years in the Framingham Heart Study, *British Medical Journal*, December 4, 2008.

CHAPTER 7

7.3 SHARE YOUR ISSUES AND PROBLEMS

1 See Wikinomics: How Mass Collaboration Changes Everything.

CHAPTER 8

8.5 UNDER PROMISE AND OVER DELIVER

1 The "Winner's Curse" was a term coined in the oil fields to describe, in the days before thorough seismic imaging, how an active oil well could lead to overinvestment by misjudging how much oil was actually in the ground. Richard Thaler, well known behavioural economist, used that same idea to describe a whole set of phenomenon that fall into the same pattern. Companies that have successive quarters of above-average expected earnings end up being unduly punished once they merely meet analysts' expectations. Seems unfair doesn't it? Perhaps, but what did the company do (or more to the point not do) to let expectations reach such high levels. Could they have done more to rein in the high notes of press and stock market opinion? Probably, so why not manage expectations instead of rising on the coat-tails of public opinion.

CHAPTER 9

9.1 MAKE YOUR EMPLOYEES HAPPY!

1 Google has long adopted the "20% rule", noted earlier, whereby 20% of an employee's time (in a given day, week, month or year) can be devoted to anything they wish to work on. Many of Google's best ideas have come from employees doing what their heart desired (i.e., Google Earth, Gmail etc.)

9.3 GIVE AND SHOW MORE TRUST

2 Remember, as renowned psychologist Barry Schwartz is fond of saying, there is no rule or incentive that has ever been devised that cannot be undone by "bad will". Likewise, "good will" saves probably more time and effort than any stringent rule ever can.

CHAPTER 12

12.2 ENCOURAGE YOUR PEOPLE TO PUT ON THE SIX THINKING HATS

1 To find out more about Professor de Bono's work visit www.debono.com or their commercial training partner de Bono Thinking Systems – www.debonothinkingsystems.com

CHAPTER 13

13.2 UNDERSTAND THE SPECIALISTS AND PLANTS OF THE BELBIN MODEL

1 To find out more about Professor Belbin's work go to www.belbin.com

CHAPTER 14

14.1 IT'S YOUR DUTY TO KICK AND PAT!

1 This was exactly the line used on professional baseball players who were being traded or sent to the minors by the general manager of the Oakland Athletics' Billy Beane (played by Brad Pitt in the 2011 film *Money Ball*). Always be respectful to the person, but also be honest about how they are performing.

2 Marcus Buckingham and Curt Coffman offer a supporting and brilliant explanation of the difference between the duties of a manager and the duties of a leader in their book *First Break All The Rules*, ©Gallup Organization.

14.2 SPREAD UNDERSTANDING OF DIFFERENT ATTITUDES AND BEHAVIOURS THROUGH MBTI

3 For more information on MBTI go to: www.myersbriggs.org

14.3 PUT YOURSELF FORWARD FOR A THREE SIXTY

4 The question of whether 360° evaluations actually work to boost output is nicely handled in a recent 2012 post on the American Psychological Associations (APA) website. In the article "Do 360° Evaluations Work?", Harriet Edleson answers her question with "yes" but goes on to argue that ". . . too often they aren't administered or followed up properly". She goes on to discuss how to boost their value.
http://www.apa.org/monitor/2012/11/360-evaluations.aspx
For more information about the Leadership Dimensions Questionnaire go to www.isolon.com

14.4 KNOW WHEN TO ADAPT OR INNOVATE

5 For more information about Dr Kirton's inventory go to: www.kaicentre .com

14.5 RECRUIT THE PERSON AND NOT THE CV/RÉSUMÉ

6 To use a sports team to illustrate the importance of recruiting and developing talent go to: http://www.linkedin.com/today/post/article/ 20130310201121-10904058-8-tips-to-building-a-championship- team?ref=email

CHAPTER 15

15.3 WATCH OUT FOR SIGNS OF STRESS

1 A great place to start is to sit down, maybe with your team, and watch the National Geographic documentary called *Stress: The Silent Killer*, http://www.pbs.org/programs/killer-stress/. Or better yet find out how much you know about stress right now by taking the National Geographic Stress Quiz found here: http://science.nationalgeographic. com/science/health-and-human-body/human-body/stress-quiz.html. In either case you and your team will come out better informed, and hence better prepared, to deal and manage stress at work.

CHAPTER 16

16.3 RETHINK THE IDEA OF INCENTIVES

1 For those of you steeped in the power of financial incentives and doubting these assertions, then I recommend you stop now and read the famous Harvard Business Review article by Steven Kerr entitled "On the Folly of Rewarding A While Hoping for B". The essence of the article, which is elicited by the title so nicely, is that organizations often (quite by accident) financially reward behaviours that they decidedly do not wish to occur. A star quarterback is given a bonus for every completed pass. So guess what: his completion rate goes up, just as incentive theory would predict, and yet he passes for fewer yards and his team scores an all-time low that season, thereby missing the playoffs. This is not made up, it really happened in the National Football League and the quarterback's name was Rob Johnston of the Buffalo Bills.

CHAPTER 19

19.2 CONSIDER IF A CHANGE OF CULTURE IS NEEDED

1 In fact research, dating back to the early 1980s, has consistently shown that the relationship between organizational culture and organizational performance is complex one, requiring lots of advance planning and understanding.

See: Alan L. Wilkins and William G. Ouchi (1983), "Efficient Cultures: Exploring the Relationship Between Culture and Organizational Performance", *Administrative Science Quarterly*, Vol. 28, No. 3, *Organizational Culture* (Sep, 1983), pp. 468–481.

http://www.jstor.org/discover/10.2307/2392253?uid=3739448&tuid=2&uid=3737720&tuid=4&sid=21101908632407

ABOUT THE AUTHORS

John Cross is neither an academic nor an ex-chief executive of a Fortune 500 company. But it is precisely that which he isn't, that makes his contributions in this book so unique and so engaging. His field of vision isn't narrow like many academics, and neither has he been preoccupied with City commentators and the media like a CEO.

Rather, he spent over 15 years as a middle manager in a number of different international companies before starting his own business in 2000, designing and delivering learning and development programmes with his co-authors.

As a result, this book describes many of his direct personal experiences and those brought to him for evaluation and comment by literally hundreds of development programme participants over the years. As a result, he has developed a deep understanding of leadership and management behaviour, ranging from the utterly brilliant to the embarrassingly weak.

John admits that he himself has displayed many examples of the latter, but gradually as the years rolled past, his conduct became more understanding of the issues and of others. He has enjoyed both failure and success, and the advice he offers, sometimes borne out of hard lessons, is designed primarily to help managers at all levels think carefully about themselves and their behaviour.

John was in Her Majesty's Armed Forces for 12 years, before joining the exciting commercial world and managing a range of different functions including, sales, marketing, call centres and service engineers. As a result, he has experienced all of the wonderful variety of challenges that a manager faces every day.

John lives near Cambridge, England with his wife Julia. They have three children and eight grandchildren.

Rafael Gomez is Associate Professor in Industrial Relations and Human Resources (University of Toronto). He currently holds a cross-appointment at Woodsworth College and the Centre for Industrial Relations and Human Resources. He received his BA in Economics and Political Science from York University (Glendon College) and an MA in Economics and PhD in Industrial Relations from the University of Toronto. Since graduating in 2000, he has gone on to work and teach at the London School of Economics as a Senior Lecturer in Management.

He has been invited to conduct research and lecture in universities and research institutes around the world, including such cities as Madrid, Moscow, Munich and Zurich. He has worked with both public and private sector organizations on various research projects and has presented his findings at over 50 national and international conferences. Professor Gomez has published in numerous journals including the *British Journal of Industrial Relations, Journal of Population Economics, Canadian Public Policy* and the *Canadian Journal of Economics.* In January 2006, he was awarded the Labor and Employment Relations Association's 2005 John T. Dunlop Outstanding Scholar Award for exceptional contributions to international and comparative labour and employment research.

He is also currently the director and co-founder of ThinkTank-Toronto (TTT), a social enterprise established in 2005, whose mandate is to document, study and promote cultural innovation in the City of Toronto and other urban locations around the globe.

Dr Kevin Money, Professor at Henley Business School is the Director of The John Madejski Centre for Reputation.

His areas of expertise are: Relationships; Organizational Reputation; Corporate Social Responsibility; Governance and Sustainability; Team Building; Executive Coaching; Leadership; Mentoring.

Kevin teaches on the MBA programme and he is a tutor on Henley's Advanced Management Programme. He also supervises DBA and PhD Research Associates.

Kevin is a Chartered Psychologist, a member of the British Psychological Society and a licensed NLP Practitioner. He is also the author of numerous academic articles and has published in outlets such as the *Journal of Business Research*, the *Journal of Business Ethics* and the *Harvard Business Manager*. Kevin is the Director of the Positive Psychology Forum and a board member of iSolon. He has acted as a consultant to major companies and voluntary organizations in the UK, USA and South Africa, and until recently was a Fellow of the Sunningdale Institute and an elected board member of the European Academy of Business in Society.

ACKNOWLEDGEMENTS

I am enormously grateful to the following authors and want to recognize the contribution that their works have made to my thinking over the past 25 years or so. I urge you to read and regularly re-read the books and articles they have crafted, often after years of painstaking research. It still surprises me that, for just a few dollars, so much value can be had for so little expense. I'm indebted to them all.

Ricardo Semler – *Maverick! The Success Story Behind the World's Most Unusual Workplace*

Tom Peters and Robert H. Waterman – *In Search of Excellence: Lessons from America's Best-run Companies*

Marcus Buckingham and Curt Coffman – *First Break All the Rules*

Daniel Goleman – *Emotional Intelligence: Why it Can Matter More Than IQ*

Daniel Goleman and Richard Boyatzis – "Social Intelligence and the Biology of Leadership." *Harvard Business Review* article, Reprint R0809E

Stephen R Covey – *The Seven Habits of Highly Effective People*

Ronald A Heifetz, Martin Linsky and Alexander Grashow – *Practice of Adaptive Leadership: Tools and Tactics for Changing Your Organization and the World: A Fieldbook for Practitioners*

Ken Blanchard and Spencer Johnson – *The One-Minute Manager*

Eric Berne – *Games People Play*

Jim Collins – *Good To Great*

Walter Isaacson – *Steve Jobs*

Vineet Nayar – *Employees First, Customers Second*

Gary Latham and Marie-Helene Budworth – *The Effect of Training in Verbal Self-guidance on the Self-efficacy and Performance of Native North Americans in the Selection Interview*

Bob Sutton – *Good Boss, Bad Boss*

Malcolm Gladwell – *The Tipping Point: How Little Things Can Make a Big Difference; Outliers: The Story of Success*

Peter Drucker – *The Essential Peter Drucker*

Edgar Schein – *Process Consultation Revisited*

John Kotter – *Leading Change; Our Iceberg is Melting*

Geoff Burch – *Resistance Is Useless*

Meredith Belbin – *Management Teams: Why They Succeed or Fail; Team Roles at Work*

Edward de Bono – *Six Thinking Hats*

Bruce Tuckman – *Forming Storming Norming Performing* model published in 1965

David K Foot – *Boom, Bust & Echo: Profiting from the Demographic Shift in the 21st Century*

Robert Cialdini – *Influence: The Psychology of Persuasion*

Henry Mintzberg – *Managing; Mintzberg on Management: Inside Our Strange World of Organizations*

Douglas MacGregor – *The Human Side of Enterprise*

Frederick Hertzberg – *Two-factor Theory*

Michael Kirton – *The Adaptor-Innovator Inventory*

The following publications have also proved extremely valuable in helping to shape my thinking:

The *Harvard Business Review, McKinsey Quarterly, Financial Times, Wall Street Journal.*

And a special "thank you" to the contributions from my friends and colleagues: John Steele, Phil Stutes, Sir Ranulph Fiennes, Richard Evans, Craig Redbond, Malcolm Diamond, Russell King, Des Lee, Nick Bizic, Tim Dunne, Stewart Davies, Steve Morgan, Brian McDermott.

INDEX